PASSAGE AND POSSIBILITY

PASSAGE
AND
POSSIBILITY

A Study of Aristotle's Modal Concepts

by

Sarah Waterlow

CLARENDON PRESS · OXFORD
1982

Oxford University Press, Walton Street, Oxford OX2 6DP

London   Glasgow   New York   Toronto
Delhi   Bombay   Calcutta   Madras   Karachi
Kuala Lumpur   Singapore   Hong Kong   Tokyo
Nairobi   Dar es Salaam   Cape Town
Melbourne   Auckland
and associates in
Beirut   Berlin   Ibadan   Mexico City   Nicosia

Published in the United States by
Oxford University Press, New York

British Library Cataloguing in Publication Data
Waterlow, Sarah
Passage and possibility: a study of
Aristotle's modal concepts.
1. Aristotle—Logic   2. Modality (Logic)
I. Title
160'.92'4   B491.L8
ISBN 0-19-824656-0

Library of Congress Cataloging in Publication Data
Waterlow, Sarah.
Passage and possibility.
Includes index.
1. Aristotle — Knowledge, Theory.   2. Modality
(Theory of knowledge) — History.   3. Knowledge,
Theory of — History.   I. Title.
B491.K6W37   1982   160   81-22459
ISBN 0-19-824656-0   AACR2

Set by Hope Services Abingdon
and Printed in Great Britain
at the University Press, Oxford
by Eric Buckley
Printer to the University

To the memory of
Sydney Waterlow
1878–1944
who cared about these things

Acknowledgement

I am indebted to Dr. Alexander Broadie of the University of Glasgow for his criticism of an earlier draft.

Contents

I

Introduction

No account of Aristotle's logic or of his metaphysics would be complete that did not include some attempt to expound his views on time and modality. I say 'attempt' because on either subject Aristotle's thoughts are amongst his least accessible. In the relevant passages we face obscurities of language and occasional dubieties of text. But the main difficulties lie not with these. Often enough the words are clear, yet their import continues to evade systematic philosophical comprehension. To some extent this is true even when Aristotle is considering time and modality as separate topics. But perhaps the most frustrating puzzles arise over various connections he draws between temporal and modal concepts. For if one thing is certain, it is that he sees necessity and possibility as related to time in ways that find no echo in the standard modern treatment of these modalities.

In particular he subscribes to some form of equivalence between the temporal quantifiers 'always' and 'at some time', and the modal operators 'necessarily' and 'possibly'. He maintains in each case one entailment that we can easily accept and another that strikes us as alien to the point of absurdity. He has no doubt that:

(A) If at some time it is the case that p, then it is possible that p;

nor that:

(B) If it is necessary that p, then it is always the case that p.

Proposition A is a truism. B might cause us hesitation on the ground that some (if not all) necessities (e.g. the mathematical) refer to a subject-matter to which it hardly makes sense to apply temporal language at all. However, if we assume the generally accepted logical equivalence of 'at some time —' with 'not always not —', and of 'possibly —' with 'not necessarily not —', then A may be recast as: 'If it is not always the case that not-p, then not necessarily not-p'; and by transposition and substitution of 'p' for 'not-p', this gives proposition B. Hence on the assumptions mentioned, B is at least as certain as A. However, as well as A and B, Aristotle also maintains in some shape or form the reverse entailments, i.e.:

(A') If it is possible that p, then at some time it is the case that p;

and

(B') If it is always the case that p, then it is necessary that p.

A' and B' are neither truistic themselves nor derivable from truisms, and to us, who find them thoroughly implausible, their plausibility to Aristotle is something of a mystery. The main object of the present work is to explain his grounds for these two curious propositions and to determine their role in his thought concerning time and modality.[1]

The texts to which I shall devote most attention are *De Caelo* I.12 and *De Interpretatione* 9. These are the major exhibits for any enquiry into the present topic, and any proposed account will be judged by its power to solve their much-debated philosophical obscurities. Among modern writings I shall be mainly concerned with Professor J. Hintikka's series of studies on the relation of modality to time in Aristotle.[2] Here he has amassed the textual evidence for Aristotle's commitment to A' and B' and has also conducted a many-sided investigation into the conceptual issues which arise. My own incursion into this thicket of interconnected

---

[1] For A' and B' see *De Caelo* I.12 *passim*. Both are supported by *Metaph*. Θ. 3, 1047a11–14, if 'ἐσήμαινεν' implies mutual entailment. For A' see *Top*. II.11, 115b17–18; *Phys*. IV.12, 221b28–29 and 222a8–9 if 'ὅσων' is read as 'of all and only those'; *Metaph*. Θ. 10, 1051b13–17. A version of A' follows from ibid. 8, 1049b17ff. *Pace* Hintikka (op. cit. below, pp. 104ff.), I hesitate to take *Metaph*. Θ.4, 1047b3ff. as evidence for A'. For B': *Phys*. III.4, 203b30; *De Gen. et Corr*. II.11, 338a1–3; *Metaph*. Θ.8, 1050b7–8, 20–21; N 2, 1088b23–25. See also *De Gen. et Corr*. II.9, 335a33–34; *Metaph*. E.2, 1026b27–28, K 8, 1064b32–33.

[2] Collected in *Time and Necessity*, Oxford 1973. All references to Hintikka are to this work.

questions has the benefit of Hintikka's previous penetration, despite divergence at certain fundamental points.

One of the few data to emerge indisputably for the texts is Aristotle's refusal to allow that literally every possibility is fulfilled. For instance: in *De Interpretatione* 9, in the course of arguing against a view which in his opinion would entail that whatever happens happens of necessity, he speaks of a coat concerning which, he says, there is the possibility of its being cut up even though it never will be, since in fact it is going to wear out first (19a12-14). Again, he sees terrestrial substances in general as liable to contrary conditions; thus a stationary object has the possibility of remaining at rest, but also of moving, and of moving in different directions. If, then, it does stay still for a given time, the possibility of its being in motion during that time goes for ever unfulfilled. The Megarians, he maintains, are wrong in holding that something can only do or be what it actually does or is. For even while a man is seated, there is the possibility of his standing and hence of not being seated[3].

There is therefore no question of a total coincidence of the possible with the actual. Nor however is there any serious room for doubting that Aristotle maintains A'. So unless at the outset we are to regard him as wildly inconsistent, we must suppose that he intends A' only in a restricted form. What is the principle of restriction? On this Aristotle does not pronounce explicitly. Hintikka believes that A' is meant to cover only general possibilities or possibilities for kinds of states of affairs or events. Thus from its being possible that coats or garments or pieces of cloth be cut or divided, it follows that something of the kind did, does or will happen at some time, but for any particular instance it does not follow. Since the possibility of this coat's being cut up depends upon its being in general possible that such a thing should occur, the possibility in any given particular case entails that in some case or other an event of the kind takes place; but it need not happen to this coat.[4] On this account, Aristotle's complaint against the Megarians centres not so

[3] *Metaph.* Θ.3.
[4] Hintikka pp. 100f., 162, 171f.

much on their general assumption that possibility implies the actuality of what is said to be possible, but on the precise form in which they maintain this. They hold that there is no possibility of X's sitting at a stated time unless he *actually is then sitting*; whereas for Aristotle this particular situation is one of a class of others like it, *some* one of which must be realized if the possibility is genuine.

I shall return to this suggestion of Hintikka's, which I outline now only in order to illustrate one way in which the evidence for Aristotle's adherence to A′ might be reconciled with the indubitable fact that for him the actual and the possible differ in extension. Meanwhile there is a prior question to be raised, whose answer will affect our view of this and every other aspect of the Aristotelian relation between time and modality. Any explanation of the meaning, the grounds, and indeed the scope of this relation will depend on *whether the connections expressed by A′ and B′ are taken as autonomous, based only on the terms which explicitly appear in these propositions; or as resting on logically extraneous assumptions*. For the present I only point to this question and the implications of a decision either way: the correct answer, as I understand it, will begin to take shape only in the fourth chapter of this study, and will not be fully substantiated until the last.

The distinction implied by the question is one which Aristotle must be presumed in general to recognize; and I assume too that if put to him he would have accepted its relevance in this particular case. If (given certain restrictions on the values of '*p*') A′ expresses an autonomous connection, then 'possibly *p*' is by itself a logically sufficient condition for 'at some time *p*'. In that case, inference from the former to the latter is comparable to the logical move (which he himself sanctions) from 'possibly *p*' to 'it is not the case that necessarily not *p*'.[5] Aristotle would, I take it, have acknowledged that there is a genuine question whether the two moves have the same kind of justification. This is not to say that he ever actually considered the matter, nor that his consideration would have yielded a definite answer, but only that the question itself cannot be ruled artificial in relation

---

[5] *De Int.* 13, 22b22-23.

to him. Thus it is legitimate for us to examine the evidence
from this point of view.

Hintikka speaks of proposition A′ as a 'bridge between
time and modality'.[6] This very image (which is also appropriate to B′) conveniently straddles the alternative interpretations outlined above. Is the gap (as we see it to be)
between the two sets of concepts closed for Aristotle because
in his view the modalities by their own logic generate a
passage to and from 'at some time . . .' and 'always . . .'? Or is
the junction effected by some independent principle or
principles, in which case it is, as we should say, synthetic,
not analytic? Since he also holds A and B, which express the
converse connections from A′ and B′, we have some kind of
biconditional relationship between 'possibly . . .' and 'at
some time . . .', and between 'necessarily . . .' and 'always
. . .'. A and B are analytically true implication-statements; so
if the same were true of A′ (within certain limits) and of B′,
it would follow that the modal operators and the temporal
quantifiers are analytically equivalent (at least within the
field where A′ holds good). We may or may not regard such
a relation as amounting quite to identity of meaning; but
there is no withstanding the conclusion that alethic modality,
on such an interpretation, is not logically independent of
non-modal concepts. Modal logic turns out to be an application of quantification theory in which the quantifiers are
taken as ranging over times.

That Aristotle should have maintained such a position or
found himself even attracted towards it would be a matter of
no small philosophical interest. Since the terms involved
apply to almost any subject-matter we should expect such a
view to exert its influence over all branches of his thought.
Hence in any given area the interpreter would need to take
this into account even if only as a latent factor, much as he
takes account of the ubiquitous distinction of matter and
form. Indeed his understanding of this too should be affected,
in so far as Aristotle spells out its meaning by means of the
concepts of actuality and potentiality. Since what is potential
is at least possible, the metaphysical contrast of matter and

[6] Hintikka, p. 102.

form would turn out to consist in a contrast between different sorts of factual statement. To say that a set of bricks b_1, b_2, b_3, etc. is 'matter' for a wall would be to say that at some time some similar objects are arranged in some similar construction. To say that b_1, b_2 etc. exhibit the 'form' of a wall would be to say that these bricks at this time are arranged as this wall. The difference is the difference between definite reference and the existential quantifier. And questions of exegesis apart, the belief that Aristotle holds or comes near to holding an analytic equivalence between modal and temporal statements would contribute to more general judgements concerning Aristotle, or else concerning modality. It was he who laid the ground for subsequent systems of modal logic by formulating a number of principles commonly endorsed without question: for instance the inter-relations of possibility and necessity expressed in the modal square of opposition, and the law that what entails the impossible is itself impossible. But to some minds, any attempt to reduce necessity and possibility to extensional terms is so preposterous that their respect for his acknowledged pioneering achievement might become mixed with a rather different attitude if it appeared that he also inclined in this other, obnoxious, direction. Whereas others, by contrast, might be encouraged by his authority to nurse their own hopes of a reductionist account.

Such upshots remain, however, hypothetical until it is shown that A′ and B′ are best understood as analytic propositions. But on this the texts provide no ready-made conclusion. For instance, Aristotle does not explicitly define the modal operators by the temporal quantifiers, nor says that such a definition would be in order. Nor on the other hand does he explicitly rule this out. And at moments he seems to treat the connection as if, like a definition, it were underived and immediate. Yet he also says things which make nonsense of this. It is not merely that scattered remarks seem to point in different directions. *De Caelo* I.12 is the longest and most systematic of all the relevant passages; and this single chapter lands the reader with conflicting impressions within the space of a few central lines. Aristotle's concern here is mainly with B′, and his object is to prove it. The details of his argument do not matter just now: they will be examined in due course. In broad terms what is astonishing is his confidence, nowhere more evident than here, in the conclusion. For to modern eyes that confidence hardly seems intelligible (let alone justified) unless he is treating B' as an *axiom*. But in that case he cannot need an *argument* by which to deduce it. He derives B', or so he thinks; but by reasoning which to most observers not only fails but fails unmistakably. How then could he be convinced of B' as a conclusion if he were not all along assuming it also as a premiss? By undertaking to argue at all he admits the need of a link between the terms 'always' and 'necessarily'; which link one might reasonably suppose could only be supplied (if at all) by some extraneous assumption, so that B' would be synthetic. Yet when the required assumption fails to appear, the argument can proceed only if B' itself is being tacitly employed in the role left empty. So it seems that after all B' functions as analytic. Either this last is Aristotle's real position and the argument is a sham in which he strives to sell a dogma by dressing it up as a rational deduction: or he himself is unaware of his tactics and is radically confused. These are the only alternatives unless there is more to the explicit premisses in *De Caelo* I.12 than meets the eye.

That is a question for full discussion later.[7] Meanwhile the mere fact that the argument of this central passage can even seem such an obvious *petitio principii* serves to illustrate the difficulty of interpreting the nature of the Aristotelian temporal–modal connections. And there are related issues infected by this doubt. Take, for instance, the question already raised concerning the scope of proposition A'. If A' is taken as stating that 'possibly p' is a logically sufficient condition for 'p at some time', then it is natural to suppose that the values of 'p' for which it holds are distinguished otherwise than by their non-formal content. For if the connection were to depend on the specific kind of event or situation depicted, it would not rest on the concept of 'possible' alone. Situations of any kind can be said to be possible, just as they can be said to occur at some time; so that if the connection

---

[7] Ch. IV below.

holds good for some kinds and not others, the reason for this must lie in some independent principle, and in that case it will not be possibility as such that entails realization at a time, but possibility together with some other factor. Hence if in fact Aristotle means A′ to express a direct logical connection between its terms, it is reasonable to infer that he marks off the values of 'p' for which this does and does not hold by reference to some topic-neutral difference, such as that between existentially quantified and singular sentences. This is Hintikka's view of the matter, and it "saves the appearances" to the extent of accommodating Aristotle's remark that the possibility of this particular coat's being cut up will never be fulfilled. But there may be other means of accommodation. If A′ is synthetic, then for all we know the coat example may be supported by considerations which apply in virtue of the sort of situation said to be possible. In that case some particular possibilities may fail to be realized not because they are particular, but because they are not of the relevant sort.

Anyone who interprets Aristotle's A′ and B′ as expressing connections unmediated by extraneous principles must have powerful reasons for doing so. For there are powerful reasons against. Any exegetical profits gained from such an account must be considerable to compensate for the strain of believing him to subscribe to a view so much at odds with common intuitions, according to which it is one question whether or not some kind of thing is possible, and another question whether it actually ever happens. The logician, it is true, can point to striking analogies between the formal relations of 'always' with 'sometimes' and of 'necessary' with 'possible'. Indeed, if the notion of 'modal operator' is spelt out in purely formal terms, the temporal pair may properly be classed as modal operators[8] along with other analogous pairs such as, for instance, 'certain' and 'probable'. It may even be convenient to speak of 'necessity' in connection with the strong, and of 'possibility' in connection with the weak, member of all such pairs. But the terms are now being used in an analogical sense. The intelligibility of this usage is no

---

[8] Cf. A.N. Prior, *Time and Modality*, Oxford 1957, pp. 12 ff.

argument at all for the intelligibility of the claim that what is possible (in the ordinary sense) must actually in some instance happen, since otherwise it would not have been even possible.

At its strongest, this claim states an identity of the concepts: possibility simply consisting in instantiation at some time, and necessity in unfailing instantiation at all times. The distinction between the necessary, the impossible and the contingent (what is neither necessary nor impossible) turns out to be a difference only of duration. The contingent is the intermittent: what sometimes is and sometimes is not; but it is not intermittent *because* contingent, since these are only two ways of saying the same thing. Nor can we say that such and such never happens because it is impossible, since if 'never' and 'impossible' mean the same, neither states a reason for the other. Necessary being and necessary truth are not different types of being and truth from their contingent counterparts, since if this were so the difference between them would not be wholly captured by the difference between 'always' and 'sometimes, sometimes not'. For 'always' only states all of what 'sometimes' states some of, and this is a difference in quantity alone.[9]

The disparity between any ordinary sense of 'possible' and 'at some time' is most apparent when we consider what is involved in voluntary agency and deliberation. On Aristotle's analysis,[10] voluntary agency presupposes the contingency of the intended result. The result is possible, but it is not necessary, since alternatives are possible too. This at any rate is how it is seen by a prospective agent, one who takes it to be in his power to determine the outcome. But to assume that alternatives are possible is not the same as to assume that each is, was or will be instantiated at some time. The agent may believe this too, and if so it is relevant as evidence for the possibility here and now, since what happens sometimes is not in general impossible, and therefore may be possible on this occasion. But 'it sometimes happens' could not be used, as in fact it is, to *support* the claim 'it is possible' if the two were identical in meaning. Nor need a potential agent consider himself to lack reasons for thinking some

[9] Cf. Hintikka pp. 102-3 on 'Aristotle's statistical model of modality'.
[10] *De Int.* 9; cf. *Eth. Nic.* III.3.

desired state of affairs S possible unless he has reason to
believe that it or something like it will or has come about. He
may take it that such a thing has never occurred before and
will not occur in the future either, unless he brings it about:
and he may not yet know, being undecided, whether he will
even attempt this. But he may still regard S as possible, and
would not therefore be counted as illogical or as not knowing
what 'possible' means.

It may be said that S, whatever it may be, is bound to resemble some actuality or other. Nothing is totally different
from anything else, so that there is no possibility of anything
absolutely new. But proposition A′ is neither controversial
nor interesting if it only states this trivial point. A′ engages
our attention because it seems to claim something more,
namely that the actual limits the range of the possible, so
that what is possible coincides in central and important
respects with what is at some time real. But as a logical
principle of general application this is plainly absurd.[11] The
inventive mind sees possibilities for artificial processes and
products whose logically inevitable resemblance in some
respects to actual objects in the natural world serves merely
to highlight their essential differences and the fact that these
differences are also possible. New things are possible, and
possible *qua* new. To reconcile this with A′ construed as an
analytic claim, one would be driven to maintain that all
possible types of art and artifice are actually realized at
some time.

An analytic interpretation of A′ and B′ is reminiscent of
Hume's reduction of causality to constant conjunction of
contiguous successive events. Yet even Hume found himself
compelled to allow that causal necessary connection implies
something more, even if the only available extra element is a
psychological impression. In effect, this was an admission
that a definition in terms of constant conjunction is at best
normative: the latter concept is the one we should employ if

---

[11] *Pace* Russell: '. . . *normally* when you say of a proposition that it is possible, you *mean* something like this: first of all it is implied that you do not know
whether it is true or false; and I think it is implied, secondly, that it is one of a set
of propositions some of which are known to be true.' ('The Philosophy of Logical
Atomism' in *Logic and Knowledge*, ed. Marsh, London 1956, p. 254. My italics.)

we were ideal Humean empiricists, but it is not our actual concept of causality. How strange if Aristotle, in general so much more sensitive to the nuances of ordinary thinking, and respectful of them, were to have equated necessity with omnitemporality without any explicit acknowledgement of the conceptual violence involved, or any attempt to mitigate it. But no apologia is forthcoming from him. Nor is it easy in Aristotle's case to see why he should have been led to adopt a position which he is apparently so heedless of the need to defend. It does not seem to follow from any of his well known doctrines. Nor is he driven by Hume's motive for the analogous reduction of causality. For Aristotle has put himself under no obligation to derive all human knowledge and concepts from impressions and ideas.

However, A' and B' apart, there is one well-documented respect in which time enters into Aristotle's modal thinking in a way which seems to show him impervious to the considerations by which we might try to justify our sense of a conceptual gulf between the modal and the extensional. I refer to his view that only future events and situations are contingent, and that what already is or has been is necessary. And similarly for statements: a statement is not contingent unless its temporal reference is to the future; if it is to the past or present the statement, if true, is necessarily so, and if false, impossible, because its contradictory in that case is true and necessary.[12] Evidently Aristotle employs the modal terms in senses radically different from those endorsed by what we may call the classical modern approach. According to the latter, the modality of a proposition depends on its meaning or on the kind of thing it says, and all propositions stating matters of fact are contingent regardless of the observer's temporal standpoint. Whereas for Aristotle, the same dated proposition may be contingent and then non-contingent as the observer's present overtakes the date in question. And when that date is in the past, the difference between necessity and impossibility seems to amount to no more than the difference between true and false. This conception of modality as dependent on fact, on whether or not something has

[12] Cf. *De Caelo* I.12, 283b12–14; *De Int.* 9; *Rhet.* III.17, 1418a4–5; *Eth. Nic.* VI.2, 1139b5–9.

happened, is the polar opposite of the view that grounds it
entirely in meaning or (to speak materially) in the nature of
whatever state of things the proposition represents. Hence we
may be disposed to take A' and B' as further evidence of a
general disregard on Aristotle's part of those intuitions which
for us dictate a fundamental differentiation between questions
of truth-value and questions of modal status. If a philosopher
can hold that certain propositions are necessary for no reason
other than that they are true, then it is perhaps no surprise
if he also equates being necessary with being always true: in
other words, if he maintains A' and B' as analytic principles.

However, to build a convincing case for the analytic interpretation of A' and B' on the basis of the indisputably Aristotelian doctrine that the past is necessary, more is required
than the observation that both positions are similarly repugnant to the standard modern view. One would need to show
in closer terms their harmony with one another; which is not
so easy.[13] And in any case, their resemblance in the respect
just mentioned hardly warrants an inductive argument to
the effect that since Aristotle holds one he is likely to hold the
other: for from one point of view they are not at all on the
same footing. To call the past necessary and the future alone
contingent echoes a pre-reflective pattern of thought whereby we view the past as fixed, setting the scene for present
action but logically beyond reach of its effects. By contrast,
the claim that 'possibly', by its very meaning, implies fulfilment at some time fails to answer to any natural intuition. If
we measure the probabilities by reference to Aristotle's well-
known reluctance to set aside common sense unless for some
good reason, rather than by his divergence from some later
academic norm, we shall be inclined to conclude that he does
not maintain A' and B' analytically.

The general alternative to the analytic interpretation is one
according to which the connections are synthetic and depend
on further concepts and principles not mentioned in A' and
B' themselves. Such an account remains no more than a blank
possibility unless specific elements in Aristotle's thinking can
be identified in support. This line of investigation has not, I

---

[13] See below, Ch. VI, pp. 124 ff.

believe, been systematically followed, perhaps because the texts provide few pointers in a profitable direction. But unless the synthetic alternative is substantiated it is uninteresting, since in the abstract it says no more than that the analytic one is wrong; whereas the latter at least assigns a definite position to Aristotle. It may partly be this fact that inclines Professor Hintikka to the analytic side on the whole. Hintikka does not explicitly oppose this to the synthetic alternative, and he emphasizes that Aristotle never defines the modalities by the temporal quantifiers.[14] But he says all the same: 'In passage after passage [Aristotle] explicitly or tacitly equates possibility with sometime truth and necessity with omnitemporal truth.' (p.151.) 'It is well-nigh axiomatic for Aristotle that possibility equals sometime truth.' (p.160.) He speaks also of 'the extensionalist account of possibility to which Aristotle resorts' (p.161), and, less positively, of factors in Aristotle's conceptual apparatus 'that tended to push him towards . . . an extensional (tense-logical) reduction of modal notions to non-modal ones' (p.113).[15]

However, Hintikka is well aware of the difficulty of believing that this is Aristotle's considered opinion. And he argues that it is not really a considered opinion at all but the result of a mistake. Aristotle uses a certain rule or method (to be examined in the next chapter) for deciding whether a given thing is possible. Hintikka suggests that Aristotle is radically confused by the terms of the method, in such a way that its application, in his hands, writes off as impossible something which never happens.[16] Thus he cannot avoid using modal concepts as if they were analytically equivalent to the temporal quantifiers, even though he is understandably reluctant to adopt this as an official principle.[17] This would certainly help to explain the ambiguity of the textual evidence, and in particular why in *De Caelo* I.12 Aristotle feels

[14] Hintikka, pp. 102-3.
[15] Cf. N. Rescher, 'On the Logic of Chronological Propositions', *Mind* LXXV, 1966, pp. 86f., who takes Aristotle as defining the modal operators by the temporal quantifiers. See also his 'Truth and Necessity in Temporal Perspective', in *The Philosophy of Time*, ed. R. Gale, London 1968, p.202.
[16] For the details of the alleged confusion see below, Ch. IV, pp. 53 ff.
[17] Hintikka (p.113) speaks of 'deep tensions that seem to have been operative in Aristotle's [sc. modal] thinking'.

the need to argue for B′ as if it were by no means obvious, while at the same time apparently using it as an underived premiss. It would also explain why he makes no effort to defend his position against the counter-claims of ordinary intuition: it is not a tenet of which he is convinced, but a trap in which he is caught; and if he were able to articulate what led him there he would not have been led.

However, Hintikka by his own language seems at moments to veer towards the synthetic approach. In particular he gives to Aristotle's A′ the title 'Principle of Plenitude'.[18] Hintikka insists that this is only a label, but the phrase has connotations which cannot easily be set aside. A.O. Lovejoy coined it to cover 'any . . . deductions from the assumption that no genuine potentiality of being can remain unfulfilled, that the extent and abundance of the creation must be as great as the possibility of existence and commensurate with the productive capacity of a "perfect" and inexhaustible Source, and that the world is better, the more things it contains'.[19] This description applies to a variety of doctrines, but it can hardly accommodate the view that 'possible' is by itself a logically sufficient condition for 'realized at some time'. For according to the Principle of Plenitude, possibilities are realized to the maximum not because they are simply possibilities, but because maximum realization is good, an expression of the perfection of the universe or its maker. Indeed the principle seems to be intended to explain why possibilities are realized, which suggests that in themselves they carry no reason why they should be. In short, it assumes a logical gap and responds by offering a mediating link based on notions of value and perfection. Hintikka implies at times that Aristotle's A′ belongs in the general tradition of doctrines of plenitude. If this is correct, A′ should be regarded as synthetic.

If through confusion Aristotle could not prevent himself from treating 'possibly' as logically sufficient for 'at some time', and yet through sound instinct could not affirm this with confidence, then perhaps he sought other, and incompatible, grounds for joining concepts which logically he was

---

[18] Hintikka, pp. 94 ff.
[19] *The Great Chain of Being*, New York 1960, p. 52.

able neither to separate nor to identify. That may be. In broad terms this is the picture which emerges from Hintikka's discussion. However, here I shall argue that on the contrary, Aristotle's position on A' and B' is much more coherent than at first sight appears, and that far from being the mass of unresolved tensions just indicated, it is a rational construction of logical and metaphysical elements. The logical side will engage our attention now.[20]

---

[20] I say nothing in this monograph of the Master Argument of Diodorus Cronus, in which modal and temporal concepts are mingled in ways reminiscent (in their oddity at least) of the Aristotelian connections. Hintikka writes: '. . . as far as the topics connected with the Master Argument are concerned, there was . . . a great deal of agreement between Diodorus and Aristotle' (p. 182; see pp. 179-213 *passim*). Whether the present findings on Aristotle bear out this view would be matter for a separate study.

II

Aristotelian modality (I)

In *Prior Analytics* I.13, 32a18-20 Aristotle writes: 'I say that the *possible* (τὸ ἐνδεχόμενον) is that which is not necessary, but which, if we suppose it the case, has no impossible consequences.'[1] Later (14, 33a24-5) he speaks as if he has given a definition ('ὁρισμός') of possibility, and the reference is probably to the former passage. Some have complained of circularity, on the ground that the quoted statement spells out one modal concept in terms of others. Aristotle would probably not be seriously disturbed. We have already seen how implausible it is to ascribe to him a *definition* of possibility in non-modal, temporal, terms. And the texts give no reason to suppose him inclined to define modal concepts in some other non-modal way. How could any such definition fail to eliminate modality altogether? No doubt he would agree that the modalities form a primitive set of concepts. If this means that in some strict sense of 'definition' they are none of them definable, so be it. His point in this and parallel passages is that they can be *explained*, by means of their mutual relations.[2]

What the sentence just quoted explicates is 'possible' in the sense of 'contingent', i.e. 'neither necessary nor impossible'. It is this sense, rather than the wider one that merely negates 'impossible', that guards the distinction between modality and fact, since without it the necessary and the not-impossible coincide with the true. Aristotle's loyalty to the distinction (in some form or other) is sufficiently proved by his ὁρισμός of contingency, and the same interest is also expressed as a particular concern to mark off the impossible from the merely false.[3] For it is by being false that a proposition best displays the fact of its not being

---

[1] Cf. *Metaph.* Θ. 4, 1047b9-11. and 3, 1047a24 ff.
[2] 'ὁρισμός' could be translated 'criterion'.
[3] Cf. *An. Pr.* I. 15, 34a 25ff., and *De Caelo* I.12, 281b2 ff. (discussed below).

necessary; hence if not impossible it is contingent. However, if false this may be because it is impossible, or again it may not, since not all falsehoods are obvious impossibilities. On the other hand, not all impossibilities are obvious. So how do we decide that a false proposition is possible, when *ex hypothesi* we lack the most obvious grounds for asserting this— namely its truth? Aristotle's answer is: *suppose* it true and see whether any impossibility follows. Thus this explanation of 'contingency' is also a principle for determining what is contingent.[4]

In the *Prior Analytics* Aristotle is not explicitly concerned with temporal properties. But in *De Caelo* I.12 we find him using the same method, only this time with a specifically temporal bearing. This is so in a double sense. In the first place, in *De Caelo* the principle of contingency comes in to subserve his main purpose in the context, which is to prove proposition B′, that what is always the case, is so necessarily. Secondly, as we shall see, the principle itself is now cast in a form that makes special reference to time. Here, then, modal and temporal concepts connect in ways unhinted at in the ὁρισμός of the *Analytics*. Since my concern here is with precisely such connections, I shall take *De Caelo* I.12 as the basis for a detailed exposition of Aristotelian modality.

This exposition will be governed by an assumption to be made explicit at the start. No one in these days will be easily won over by the *De Caelo* argument for B′. It seems that it must be radically astray, for from the premiss '*p* always' how could it possibly follow that '*p*' is necessary? However, it is not so easy as some critics have thought to locate the fault. Yet until this is done, every element in the argument is open to doubt, including the principle of contingency on which Aristotle here relies. On the other hand, so far as this simply coincides with the ὁρισμός of the *Prior Analytics*, it is hardly up for question, it being as clear as anything could be[5] that

---

[4] By calling it a 'ὁρισμός' he implies that this is the only method for discovering impossibilities that are not obvious from the outset, and also that it needs no justification. In other words, he would simply reject the sceptical question 'How do you know that there might not be latently impossible propositions whose impossibility is not even displayed in their consequences?'

[5] Abstractly speaking, that is. Chrysippus produced a counter-example (see W. and M. Kneale, *The Development of Logic*, Oxford 1962; pp. 126-8), which

a non-necessary proposition is possible if and only if from the supposition of its truth nothing impossible follows. This formal statement rests on the law that if 'p' entails 'q' and 'p' is necessary, then so is 'q'. However, as I have indicated, in *De Caelo* I.12 Aristotle temporalizes the principle in a way which may or may not be defensible. The "pure" dictum of the *Analytics* gives no assurance that this extension is legitimate, nor affords any clue as to its reason. Hence it is not certain *a priori* that the temporal component of the *De Caelo* version is not a source of fallacy in Aristotle's proof of B'.

However, I propose for the present to expound the temporalized principle on the assumption that it is coherent. This will not be fully justified until the fourth chapter, where I shall argue that the trouble in the *De Caelo* argument for B' is to be traced to other, conceptually isolable, factors. Meanwhile I shall ignore the shadow of doubt cast by the strange result to which, in this context, the temporalized principle contributes. It will be necessary from time to time to refer for illustrative purposes to the particular application by which that result is reached. But I shall make these allusions as brief as possible, since they stir up problems which, if I am right, are strictly extraneous to our present concern with the principle itself.

Whereas in the *Analytics* Aristotle spoke of the possible as '$τὸ\ ἐνδεχόμενον$', in *De Caelo* I.12 he says '$τὸ\ δυνατόν$'. Here too he is evidently concerned with contingency rather than the mere denial of impossibility consistent with 'necessary'. For his purpose is to establish and then deploy a distinction between the *false* (hence not necessary) and the impossible. He begins with the announcement (281b2–3): ' "False" and "impossible" do not mean the same.' He then notes a further distinction:

The impossible and the possible, the false and the true, may be hypothetical ($ἐξ\ ὑποθεσέως$), as for instance when we say that if a certain condition holds, it is impossible that the triangle should have two right angles, and that if a certain condition holds, the diagonal is commensurate [*sc.* with the sides of the square]. On the other hand, things may

is "verbal" in the sense that the natural response is not to question the rule but to seek to classify the fallacy.

be possible and impossible, false and true, *simpliciter* (ἁπλῶς). (281b3-8.)

Now he returns to the initial theme:

Now for something to be false *simpliciter* is not the same as for it to be impossible *simpliciter*. For to say that you, who are not standing, are standing, is false but not impossible. Similarly, to say that a man is singing, when he is playing the lyre but not singing, is false but not impossible. But that someone is standing and sitting at the same time, and that the diagonal is commensurate, is not only false but also impossible. So to suppose what is false is not the same as to suppose what is impossible. An impossible consequence follows from what is impossible. (281b8-15.)

By this last remark Aristotle does not mean that the impossible implies only what is impossible. That would be a blunder, at any rate by latter-day formal notions of implication. He means, rather, that if '*q*' is a consequence of '*p*' and '*q*' represents an impossibility, then so does '*p*'; whereas if and only if nothing impossible follows from '*p*', we are entitled to regard '*p*' as meaning something possible. This is precisely the principle stated in *Prior Analytics* I.13, 32a18-20. And in arguing for his main conclusion (that what is always the case is necessary), Aristotle shows that here too he relies on the principle to provide him with a method for determining the possible.

We may note that this method is effective only if an impossible consequence (should there be one) is obviously impossible, and more obviously so than the supposition which implies it. For if the supposition were itself an obvious impossibility, there would be no need of a method to decide its status; while if all the consequences were only dubiously impossible, the method would have to be applied to them, and so on *ad infinitum* with no definite result. Aristotle's main application in *De Caelo* I.12 illustrates this point well, if we may ignore the independent problems it raises. For here the supposition whose possibility is to be upheld or refuted is that a certain state of affairs M does not obtain. This supposition is false, because *ex hypothesi* M is held to exist for ever. But it is by no means obviously impossible. Yet from it Aristotle derives (as he thinks) an explicit contradiction, that the same thing both is and is not at the same time (20-5).

But before proceeding to this important application, Aristotle illustrates what he has said so far, and it is here that the special connection between time and possibility begins to appear.

A man has at the same time the possibility (ἅμα ἔχει τὴν δύναμιν) of being seated and of standing, because when he has the one possibility he has the other also: but not in such a way that he can be standing at the same time as sitting, but only at another time. (281b15–18).

The example is taken up from earlier, where he said: 'To say that you, who are not standing, are standing, is false but not impossible.' (9–10.) It is shown not to be impossible by the method of supposition. This much is clear. But what are we to make of the reference to 'another time'?

At first sight it seems that Aristotle is simply pointing out that contrary possibilities cannot be realized at once. But there is more to it than this, as appears if we follow him into his proof that what is always the case is so of necessity. His reasoning, briefly, is as follows: let it be the case that p always. Now suppose that not-p. This supposition entails an absurdity. For, he says, if true it would have to be true 'at another time', i.e. at a time other than that in which p obtains. But there is no other time than this, *ex hypothesi*. Hence if we suppose that 'not-p' is true, we must suppose it true at a time when *ex hypothesi* it is false. Hence we cannot suppose it true except at a time at which its falsity is understood as given. Thus the supposition is impossible. (18ff.)

At present, as I have said, I am not concerned to diagnose the weakness of this argument, for I am assuming that whatever its faults, they do not extend to the concept of possibility on which it rests. All that now matters is the light thrown on that concept itself. What emerges is this: firstly we start with the fact, taken as known, that 'p' (an undated proposition in the present tense[6]) is true for a certain time. Secondly, its concurrently false contradictory, 'not-p', is said not to be possible unless there is a time when 'not-p' may be supposed true which does not coincide with the time when it is known to be false. Where it is taken as known that p is

---

[6] On Aristotle's 'tendency to take temporally indefinite sentences as paradigms of all informative sentences' see Hintikka, Ch. IV.

always the case, there is no other time, and 'not-p' is automatically rejected as representing an impossibility. But now apply this to a case where it is known that p, but not that p always obtains: for instance, Aristotle's example of the man who is sitting. In this case the truth of the supposition that he is not sitting (because, say, standing) may be referred without contradiction to a time beyond that in which he is known to be sitting. Thus we have no reason to say that the not-sitting or the standing is impossible, and are therefore entitled to consider it possible.

Here we have what I have called the temporalized version of the *Analytics* principle of possibility. According to the latter, a false proposition 'p' is possible (contingent) if and only if nothing impossible follows from supposing it true. According to the temporalized version, a false 'p' is possible (contingent) if and only if nothing impossible follows from supposing it *true at a time other than the time when it is false*.

In the light of this let us return to Aristotle's earlier quoted remark, that a man has at the same time the possibilities both of standing and of sitting, but only so as to realize them at different times. We can now see that more lies behind this than the principle that contraries cannot be simultaneously realized in the same subject. No doubt that is part of what he has in mind, if only because it is a truism common to all theories of possibility. But there is also the further and special principle that if we wish to ascertain that a currently sitting man (whose actual posture shows him to have the *possibility* of sitting) has also the possibility of standing, then we must convince ourselves that nothing impossible follows from supposing him to be standing (or: from supposing 'He is standing' to be true) at some other time. This special principle is liable to be confused with the first, truistic, one, because both are concerned with the possibility of contraries, and both involve reference to different times. But they differ in that the first governs the assertion that such and such a possibility is realized, while the second governs the assertion that such and such is a possibility. That is to say: according to the first, if we (a) hold that a situation S actually obtains at t, and (b) have established, by whatever means and in whatever sense, that a contrary situation T is possible, then we are not entitled to assert that T *is realized* unless we assign the realization to some time other than *t*. Whereas according to the second principle, if we hold that S actually obtains at *t*, then we are not entitled to assert that its contrary T *is possible* unless we have ascertained that nothing impossible follows from supposing T realized at some time other than *t*.

At this point a brief summary. Three principles have so far emerged as governing Aristotle's argument in *De Caelo* I.12. They are as follows:

(i)   Contrary situations cannot be realized simultaneously.

(ii)   Even though '*p*' is false, '*p*' is possible if and only if for all *q*, if '*q*' follows from '*p*', '*q*' is not impossible.

(iii)   Even though '*p*' is false at *t*, '*p*' is possible if and only if for all *q*, if '*q*' follows from ' "*p*" is true at some time $t' \neq t$', then '*q*' is not impossible.

The second of these is the principle for determining possibility which Aristotle lays down in the *Prior Analytics*. The third is this principle temporalized. In fact, the second can only be said to appear in *De Caelo* I.12 in so far as the third does: it is present as that of which the third is a version.

The first two are fundamentally required by any theory of modality. But (iii) is not such a requirement. If it were, there would be no sense of 'possible' that could be applied without reference to (iii). But at least one such sense is generally recognized, viz. purely logical possibility (self-consistency). Given that X is sitting at *t*, we can establish the logical possibility of his standing without considering what follows from supposing this to be a fact at a time other than *t*. It is enough if we can satisfy ourselves that no impossibility follows from supposing it to be a fact at any time whatever: even, for instance, at *t* itself—our supposition in this case being the counterfactual one that X was standing rather than sitting at a time when really he was sitting.

It is the third principle, then, that distinguishes Aristotle's *De Caelo* concept of possibility from at least some others. But to have said this is not yet to have explained it. Granted that for him 'possible' does not mean 'logically possible', what does it mean? Moreover, in view of the contrast just drawn between the first two principles and the third, another explanation now seems called for. Since the latter does not apparently embody a universally self-evident requirement, why does Aristotle put it forward as a principle?

Let us probe (iii) further. We meet it in the pages of Aristotle, not of a modern symbolic logician. So we do not find it presented in formal notation designed to eliminate the ambiguities of natural language. For instance, if we want to know whether some false proposition '*p*' is possible, (iii) tells us to scan for absurdity the consequences of supposing it true 'at another time'. But as it stands this is not a clear instruction. What exactly is the premiss whose consequences we are to regard as relevant? Is it simply ' "*p*" is true at some other time'? Or is it the conjunction of this with another proposition whose inclusion in the premiss Aristotle assumes as needing no declaration? A study of his wording will not decide the question. In English we do not reserve the terms 'follows', 'consequence' and their associates for only those inferences where all the premisses are made explicit, and there is no reason to think that Aristotle rigidly observed such a rule with his Greek equivalents.

Does it make sense to interpret (iii) as concerned with the consequences of the isolated supposition that '*p*' holds good at some other time? It is true that such paradigm cases of contingency as 'John is standing' would turn out possible by such a test. But this hardly supports the above interpretation unless it is also shown that those cases would turn out impossible on any other. Moreover, we may well wonder about the point of the method thus understood. Why, in particular, is there any need to refer to a time other than that in which '*p*' happens to be false? For if possibility is established by seeing what follows from the simple supposition that '*p*' is true at some different time, why can it not equally well be established by seeing what follows from the counterfactual supposition that '*p*' (rather than some contrary) is true at the very time when in fact it is false?

Let *t* be a time when '*p*' is false. In themselves, the suppositions (1) '*p* at *t*' and (2) '*p* at some time *t'* ≠ *t*' differ only in the time-indicator. There seems to be no reason why, if each is considered in turn as an isolated premiss, either should yield or not yield impossible consequences not matched by the other. Nor is there any reason to think that in either case the possibility or impossibility of the consequences would be easier to discern than in the other.

Thus if (iii) is interpreted as concerned with the consequences of a supposition on its own, it hardly deserves to rank as a principle. For its distinctive feature, namely the reference of the suppositional truth to 'another time', turns out to be pointless. So (iii) is arbitrary and to that extent irrational. In that case we ought to reject as incoherent any conception of possibility that treats this as a principle. For the time being, however, we are working on the assumption that Aristotle's conception is not incoherent. Since for him (iii) *is* a principle, we are bound for the moment to reject an account that would render it absurd.

I therefore take this rule as concerned with the consequences of a set of premisses comprising (a) the supposition that '*p*' (in fact false at *t*) is true at some other time, and (b) some other proposition. The latter, I suggest, is a description of the state of things at *t* which includes the fact that some contrary of '*p*' is true. On this interpretation, (iii) lays it down that the man sitting at *t* has the possibility of standing if and only if from the supposition that he stands at another time, together with a statement of the facts at *t*, no impossibility follows. In other words, the possibility thus tested for is *possibility-given-the-state-of-things-at-t*. This makes excellent sense of the reference to 'another time'. If the possibility in question is possibility-given-the-state-of-things-at-a-time, and if the proposition to be tested by this method is false at the time, then in supposing it true we land ourselves with a set of premisses that cannot fail to yield a contradiction—unless it is understood that what is supposed true is supposed true *at a different time*. In short, without this temporal reference, no currently false proposition has the faintest chance of being proved possible, since the fact that it is false would mean that in supposing it true we automatically set up the premisses for a contradiction.

We can now make precise the sense in which (iii) is a version of (ii). The latter was the general rule, cited in the *Analytics*, that '*p*', though false, is possible provided that the supposition of its truth has no impossible consequences. It is assumed that this rule can give positive results, i.e. that some false propositions turn out to be possible in accordance with it. Now if 'possible' in (ii) is construed as 'possible given the state of things at a certain time', and if the time mentioned is identified with the time when 'p' is false, it follows that (ii) can only retain its power to give positive results if the supposition of truth is referred to another time. Thus (ii) becomes (iii).

Let me review the discussion thus far. In *Posterior Analytics* I.13 Aristotle characterizes the possible by a clear and cogent principle. In *De Caelo* I.12 he uses a somewhat similar one, but with a curious reference to 'another time'. The point of this is fully explained on the hypothesis that in *De Caelo* I.12 he is dealing with possibility-given-the-state-of-things-at-a-time. This hypothesis also displays the *De Caelo* principle as a rational projection from that of the *Analytics*. I therefore now take the hypothesis as established. However, this temporalized notion of possibility has so far emerged only in outline. We must consider its structure and bearings in detail.

For a sharper focus let us pursue the contrast with the familiar (to us) concept of logical possibility (self-consistency). Firstly, to establish that a false proposition is logically possible, no reference need be made to matters of fact. For even if it is shown that 'p' in conjunction with true factual premisses entails a contradiction, it does not follow that 'p' is logically impossible unless the contradiction would have arisen from 'p' alone. Whereas the sort of possibility with which Aristotle operates in *De Caelo* I.12 applies to 'p' (if false) only in so far as this is considered together with a set of true factual propositions. Secondly, as has already been said, a proposition such as 'X is standing', if known to be false at t, can as easily be seen to be logically possible by supposing it true at t as by supposing it true at any other time. Thirdly, where logical possibility is concerned, not only is there no need to refer the supposed truth to any particular time, but the possibility itself does not belong in time. The logical possibility of Julius Caesar's having lived to be eighty years old does not belong in the first century BC, nor in any other period of time. But at 281b15 Aristotle says that the man now seated *has* (present tense) the possibility of standing, and there is reason to think that he means the present tense literally. It is not merely that the man now has certain actual characteristics in virtue of which it is possible that he should be standing; the possibility itself is also a present fact. For if possibility is considered in relation to an actual state of affairs, it is natural to assign the possibility a time: that of the state of affairs. On this conception, the supposed *realization* of what is possible relative to S (but false in S) is referred to another time; but the *possibility* of the realization shares the time of S. In establishing what is possible relative to S, we establish what is possible *when* S obtains.

That this is Aristotle's meaning is clear from the text, but it raises a problem. If a man is sitting at *t*, then if, given the facts at *t*, there is no impossibility in supposing him standing at another time, we are allegedly entitled to say that at *t* he has the possibility of standing. However, given the same facts it is absurd to suppose him standing at *t* itself. Thus his standing at *t* itself is under the circumstances impossible at *t*. To say this is as much as to say that given the facts at *t*, his standing is not a possibility realizable at *t*. But how then can it make sense to say, on whatever grounds, that at *t* he has the possibility of standing? For this would imply that he has the possibility at a time when that same possibility cannot be realized: not merely is not, but cannot be. But a possibility which cannot be realized is not a possibility. Hence if we speak about a time when a so-called possibility cannot be realized, we are speaking, it would seem, about a time when the possibility does not obtain. In that case it is surely not after all legitimate to say of the man sitting at *t* that he *has then* the possibility of standing, even granted that given the facts at *t*, no absurdity results from supposing him standing at another time. Hence it would be in general illegitimate to say that the possibility of '*p*' exists or obtains at any time when some contrary of '*p*' is true. In short, if we insist on assigning not only realizations of possibilities but the possibilities themselves to times, we appear to be left with the conclusion that possibilities obtain only at those times when they are not not-realized. Thus if Aristotle assigns possibilities to times, he subverts his own efforts to uphold the non-coincidence of the false with the impossible. For that assignment (it has just been argued) entails that *when* 'p' is false, *then* it is also impossible.[7]

If Aristotle's position is as we described it earlier, he has an effective reply. According to that position, to say that 'p', though false at *t*, is possible at *t*, is to say that a set of premisses comprising (a) the supposition that 'p' is true at some other time, and (b) a description of the state of things at *t*, has no impossible consequence. This entails that 'p' is not possible at *t* if and only if there is no other time such that given (b), no impossibility follows from supposing 'p' true at it. Now take the case of the man sitting at *t*. It is perfectly true that given this fact, he cannot realize, at *t*, his possibility of standing. But this does not entail that he does not *then have* the possibility. That would be the case if and only if the state of things at *t* were such as to rule out its *ever* being true that he stands. But this does not follow from the proposition that at *t* things are such that he cannot *then* realize the possibility of standing.

Alternatively, we might say that what (under the circumstances) the man cannot realize at *t* is the possibility of standing-at-*t*. And this possibility he does not in any sense have at *t*. For if he is sitting at *t*, this fact rules out its ever being the case that he stands-at-*t*. But although at *t* he lacks the possibility of standing-at-*t*, he does not then lack the possibility of standing as such. It is true that when he realizes this possibility he will do so at a particular time, say $t + 1$. But the possibility previously unrealized and then realized is not that of standing-at-$t + 1$, but of standing as such. We may grant the critic's point that if a so-called possibility is incapable, at a given time, of being realized, it is not a possibility that genuinely obtains at that time. But this point applies only to such time-indexed possibilities as the possibility of X's standing-at-*t*. Or, more precisely, it applies to those of them that are in fact unrealized, so that only when

[7] Without symbolic notation it is easy to overlook the mistake in the argument (it is in the inference from 'is not a possibility realizable at *t*' to 'is not, at *t*, a (realizable) possibility'). Perhaps this was how the Megarians reached the position which Aristotle ascribes to them in *Metaph.* Θ.3.

realized are they possibilities. On this level the line between falsity and impossibility indeed drops away, and modal and extensional logic collapse into one another. But the possibility of standing as such, if unrealized at t, is not on that account incapable, at t, of being realized.[8] It is simply incapable of realization-at-t. But if capable, at t, of being realized at all, then it obtains at t as a genuine possibility. Thus there are still cases where what is false is nonetheless possible, and, moreover, possible *when* it is false.

We have now shown two ways in which the *De Caelo* concept of possibility relates to time. On the one hand, *what* is claimed to be possible is shown to be so by way of supposing it actual at another time; and on the other hand, the *possibility* of what is possible is itself a temporal fact. With this interpenetration of time and modality, the special structure of time itself can hardly fail to have an impact on Aristotle's temporalized possibility. Does, for instance, the famous "unidirectionality" of time (whatever exactly this means) entail a corresponding unidirectionality of possibility? We may put the question more precisely as follows. Given that 'p', though false at t, is possible then if and only if the supposition of its truth at another time is not (granted the facts at t) absurd: should we take 'another time' as covering indifferently times pastwards and futurewards from t, or is its range only in one direction? Notoriously, Aristotle's usual answer is that it ranges only over future times; there are no unfulfilled possibilities now of earlier happenings.[9] How, if at all, this principle is grounded in his concept of temporalized possibility is far from clear. The question will be considered in a later chapter.[10] But meanwhile it is worth pointing out its connection with another question, one which has probably plagued the reader throughout most of the discussion so far.

Is possibility for Aristotle a property of propositions or statements, or of what these represent, depict or describe? In other words, is 'possibly' to be understood as 'possibly true'

---

[8] Cf. *De Int.* 9, 19a23–7, discussed below, Ch. V, pp. 89f.; *Metaph.* Θ. 4, 1047 b9–11.

[9] See above, p. 11, note 12.

[10] Ch. VI.

or as 'possibly actual'? Aristotle's phraseology not only affords no answer but suggests that he does not care about the difference. For instance, in the *De Caelo* passage under investigation, he moves easily and without comment from one level of discourse to the other. At one moment he is saying that what is false may still be possible, at another he speaks of the man as having the possibility of standing. So far these slidings have not mattered, because the structure of possibility as so far presented can be reproduced on either level. The non-absurdity of the supposition may be taken as proving a proposition possibly true or an extra-linguistic state of affairs possibly real. And just as dateless present-tensed propositions are true-at-a-time, so they may be said to be possible-at-a-time; but alternatively we may think of possibility-at-a-time as belonging somehow in the world. However, this correspondence breaks down as soon as we ask about the temporal position of 'the other time'. For given that X is sitting at t, there seems to be no more difficulty in supposing 'X is standing' to have been true earlier than to be going to be true later. After all, if he actually was standing earlier, then the supposition that he was cannot entail any absurdity in conjunction with a true description of the facts at t. It seems then that on the propositional level possibility belongs both ways in time. But if we consider whether the man "has the possibility" of standing, the knowledge that he was standing once would not be conclusive grounds for a positive answer. At most it would supply evidence for one. But such evidence would be overriden if we also knew that the present state of things is such that it is absurd to suppose that it will ever be true later that he stands. If this is how things are, then he does not now have the possibility. The reason is that he now has the possibility of standing only if he now has the possibility of *coming to be* in a standing position: but something can come to be only what it will be, not what it was. Hence since on the extra-linguistic level what is possible is only what can come to be, the possibilities at t must be possibilities for future states of things. We may therefore hazard a guess that despite Aristotle's lack of concern in many passages about the proper level of discourse for possibility, his doctrine that it applies only to the future points to a fundamental preference for the level of things, not propositions. But a full discussion of this must wait.[11] Meanwhile we shall simply take it as stipulated that when a proposition is tested for possibility in accordance with principle (iii), the reference of its supposed truth is always to a later time.

We have now traced the internal structure of Aristotle's concept of possibility relative to an actual state of things. It is time to re-open the question of its coherence. One indirect reason for refusing to take this for granted lies, we saw, in the fact that the concept is crucial to a suspect piece of logic, viz. the *De Caelo* proof that 'always' entails 'necessarily'. However this ground for mistrust collapses if, as I hope to show, the twist in that argument lies elsewhere. But this cannot save the concept's credibility if a direct and independent attack can be successfully launched. To one such objection we now turn.

---

[11] See Chs. VI and VII.

III

Aristotelian modality (II)

We have been examining the concept of relative temporalized possibility (RT-possibility) which Aristotle propounds and uses in the *De Caelo* I.12 proof. The rule for this (the RT rule) lays it down that '*p*' even if false at *t*, is nonetheless possible then if and only if: the actual state of things at *t* is such that from a description of this, together with the supposition that '*p*' will be true at some later time, there follows no impossible consequence.[1] And by implication: if and only if such a consequence does follow, then '*p*' is impossible at *t*. I shall call the propositions ' "*p*" is possible/impossible at *t*' the RT-*results* (positive and negative), and the clauses following 'if and only if' the RT-*conditions*. We have dealt repeatedly with Aristotle's own example of possibility-at-*t*. An example of impossibility-at-*t* would be the impossibility of X's ever later being adolescent, given that at *t* he is already mature.

In this chapter I shall be concerned with two questions not yet considered. First, what is the logical relation between the RT-conditions and their corresponding results that justifies an inference from the former to the latter? Any doubt on this score must also extend to the modal expressions appearing in the results. For they express concepts which Aristotle has explained (even if not defined) by the claim that their application is determined by the RT-conditions. So unless the results are validly generated from the conditions, the modal concepts in the former embody a fallacy and must be regarded as incoherent. I shall begin by considering a specific objection which might be brought against the RT rule under this head. The second question is to do with the modal concepts employed in the RT-conditions themselves. What are these, and how related to those in the results? In each condition

---

[1] Cf. S. McCall, 'Time and the Physical Modalities', *Monist* 53, 1969, pp. 426 ff.

there is a reference to 'impossible' consequences, and to these consequences as 'following' or 'not following' ('συμβαίνει', *De Caelo* I.12, 281b15 and 23-5). I take it that by 'following' Aristotle means a connection such that the premisses *necessarily* (in some sense) imply the conclusion. Thus in two places in each condition there occurs either 'impossible' or its contrary. It is to be observed that nothing in our previous discussion indicates that any particular date should be assigned to these operators.

First, however, let us consider how the RT-conditions give rise to the corresponding results. Those results with which Aristotle is mostly concerned in *De Caelo* I.12 are unconditioned affirmations of possibility and impossibility, the truth of which is related to the actual state of things, as opposed to statements to the effect that such and such *would* be impossible/possible, *if* such and such a situation *were* to obtain. Near the beginning of the chapter he distinguishes in general between 'categorical' and 'on-a-hypothesis':

The impossible and the possible, the false and the true, may be hypothetical, as for instance when we say that if a certain condition holds, it is impossible that the triangle should have two right angles, and that if a certain condition holds, the diagonal is commensurate. On the other hand, things may be possible and impossible, true and false, *simpliciter*. Now for something to be false *simpliciter* is not the same as for it to be impossible *simpliciter*. (281b3-9)

It is in connection with this difference, between the false and the impossible *simpliciter*, that he now goes on to introduce the RT principle as the criterion for distinguishing them in a given case.

The parallel here of the modalities with 'true' and 'false' is instructive. It goes beyond the fact that sentences formed with both kinds of operator may be used both to make assertions and to express the unasserted consequents of hypothetical statements. In this respect the Aristotelian modalities behave like our own more familiar absolute logical possibility and impossibility. But the former also distinctively resemble 'true' and 'false' (as applied to undated sentences) in that in each case a date can be attached to the operator, and the resulting proposition depends for its truth on the state of the world at that date. Because of this, in neither case do the propositions carry the implication that they themselves would have been true no matter what the actual state of things might have been. If '*p*' is logically possible/impossible, then given any situation you like, it is logically possible or impossible that *p*, and would be so even if the given situation did not hold. But this is not in general the case with truth and falsity. 'It is true at *t* that *p*' is an unconditioned assertion, but it does not imply that '*p*' would have also been true at *t* had the actual state of things then been different. It is the same with possibility/impossibility-at-*t*. If '*p*' is impossible at *t*, this is because of the state of things at the time, and there is no guarantee that had this been different, '*p*' would still then have been impossible. This logical similarity between 'true' and 'false' and the Aristotelian modalities may encourage those inclined to interpret Aristotle as committed to a position in which modal is merged with extensional logic. If on the other hand he is not thus committed, it may have been precisely this resemblance and the consequent danger of confusion that especially spurred him to formulate a principle by which to distinguish 'false' and 'impossible'.

Let us say that the state of affairs obtaining at a time characterizes that time. Then the possibility/impossibility of '*p*' belongs to that time *qua* characterized thus. The modalities stand to the time as capacities and incapacities to a substance. It is because a substance has such and such actual properties that it can or cannot do so and so: the paper can ignite because dry. Just so, a time has its possibilities and impossibilities because of what there is at the time. It is notorious that Aristotle uses the same words ('δύναμις' and cognates) to speak of the powers, capacities and potentialities of substances. The analogy just drawn may help to explain why he seldom feels the need to indicate the difference between these concepts.[2]

Thus the modal statements with which we are now concerned are (a) unconditioned assertions, as opposed to being unasserted consequents of a hypothesis. But (b) if true, they

---

[2] He distinguishes them at *Metaph.* Δ.12, 1019b21 ff.

are not true unconditionally, i.e. in such a way as to have been automatically true even under conditions different from those in which they are. Finally, in surveying the relations between these statements and "conditionhood", we should mention (c) that the Aristotelian modal operators are not in general applied to conditional propositions; i.e. the statements are not in general of the form 'possibly/impossibly (if p then q)'. The one which especially occupies Aristotle in *De Caelo* I.12 is of the form 'impossibly p', where 'p' is a simple proposition. In this too there is a difference between Aristotle's RT-determined impossibility, and modern logical impossibility, and a parallel between the former and truth or falsity. For logical impossibility attaches only to complexes, whereas for Aristotle, a proposition need not be complex to represent an impossibility, any more than to represent a falsehood.

But while the parallels with truth and falsity, and with capacity and incapacity, may help to make 'It is possible/impossible at t that p' seem intelligible, more is needed to secure these modal concepts against the objection about to be raised. This focusses on the legitimacy of establishing such statements by means of the RT rule. Now the positive RT-condition (for possibility) seems to give no difficulty. There seems to be no harm in saying that when things at t are such as not to rule out its ever later being the case that p, then 'p' is possible then. In ordinary discourse we often say, e.g., 'It is now possible that p' under just such conditions. We also say 'It is now impossible that p' under opposite conditions, but this, though equally familiar, is not so obviously innocuous. For according to the objection, it is only through a fallacy that the negative RT-condition appears to yield this result. But if the derivation of the negative result from the negative condition breaks down, then so does the general notion of modality-at-a-time as determined by the rule. Hence even if the RT-determined 'possible at t' passes muster on its own, it is coherent only by accident, in so far as it belongs to a group of concepts one of which, it is alleged, is formed by logical trickery.

The objection is as follows. Let 'q' be the description of the facts at t, and let 'Fp' mean 'It will be the case that p at some future time', where 'future' is relative to the t mentioned in connection with 'q'. (For simplicity we may take 't' as 'now', in which case 'Fp' = 'It will be (*simpliciter*) the case that p'.) Let 'r' stand for the consequences of '(q/t & Fp)'. According to the rule for RT, the result:

(1) Imposs/$t(p)$

follows from the condition:

(2) q/t & $[\text{Nec}((q/t \ \& \ Fp) \supset r) \ \& \ \text{Imposs}(r)]$.

From (2) we derive

(3) q/t
(4) $\text{Nec}((q/t \ \& \ Fp) \supset r)$
(5) $\text{Imposs}(r)$.

From (4) and (5) respectively we have:

(6) $\text{Nec}(\sim r \supset \sim (q/t \ \& \ Fp))$

and:

(7) $\text{Nec}(\sim r)$.

By the principle that what is necessarily implied by a necessary proposition is itself necessary, (6) and (7) give:

(8) $\text{Nec}(\sim(q/t \ \& \ Fp))$.

Hence:

(9) $\text{Nec}(q/t \supset \sim Fp)$

which entails:

(10) $q/t \supset \sim Fp$.

By *modus ponens* (10) and (3) give:

(11) $\sim Fp$.

But (11) is not a modal proposition, and says only that 'p' never will be the case, not that it is impossible; whereas the desired conclusion was the modal (1). (2) does of course imply that the complex '(q/t & Fp)' is impossible, but, again, this is not what was wanted.

Continuing the objection: the most that can be said in

favour of the move from (2) to (1) is that if we treat (1) as meaning something rather different from what it seems to, then it is justified. For instance it might be suggested that we read the modal expression in (1) not as a genuine sentence-forming modal operator, but as synonymous with 'therefore', so that (1) means: (1') 'Therefore not-Fp as from t'. This expresses a legitimate inference for whoever asserts (2). Or (1) might be read as: (1'') 'We are entitled to assert that not Fp as from t'. (1'') is a deontic modal proposition in so far as it says that an assertion is logically permissible. However, this is not in fact the same as what (1) says if (1) is taken at face value. In the first place, (1'') does not follow from (2) but only from a proposition or contextual indication to the effect that (2) is asserted. But on this basis, (1'') does not entail 'not-Fp' (but only that this may be asserted, i.e. (1'') itself); whereas 'It is impossible at t that p', if it means anything, must surely entail that from t onwards it will never be the case that p. Secondly, (1) contains a double reference to t, one implicit in the meaning of 'Fp', the other attached to 'It is impossible that . . .'. And as we have seen, the impossibility of 'p' (given q) belongs at t precisely because 'q' is true at t. Now in (1'') there is no place for any reference to t apart from that contained in 'Fp'. In particular, 't' does not belong with the deontic operator in (1'') as it does with the operator in (1). For there is no particular time at which more than others it is logically permissible to assert that not Fp: or at any rate such a time is not determined by the time of 'q' mentioned in the premiss for (1''). And the same would be true if we attached a time reference to the 'Therefore' in (1').

In short, the objection continues, the claim that (2) justifies (1) cannot be upheld by equating (1) with (1') or (1''), for they are not what (1) means. But meaning what it does, its derivation from (2) seems clearly fallacious. And (it might be argued) the nature of the fallacy is obvious. Someone who lacks the benefit of symbolic notation could easily overlook the difference between 'If ϕ, it follows necessarily that ψ', and 'If ϕ, it follows that ψ necessarily'. The operator is illicitly displaced, with the result that *necessitas consequentiae* appears to be transformed into *necessitas consequentis*. Thus Aristotle probably convinced himself that (2) is a ground for (1) by first arguing validly from (2) to:

(9) $\mathrm{Nec}(q/t \supset {\sim}Fp)$

and from this, by the confusion mentioned, to:

(12) $q/t \supset \mathrm{Nec}({\sim}Fp)$.

For given that:

(3) q/t

modus ponens on (12) yields:

(13) $\mathrm{Nec}({\sim}Fp)$

or in other words:

(14) $\mathrm{Imposs}(Fp)$.

And although this is not quite the same as (1) $(\mathrm{Imposs}/t\,(p))$, it may well seem as near as makes no difference.

I shall reply to this objection by arguing first that Aristotle's move from (2) to (1) cannot be explained by reference to the fallacy suggested. He may or may not have been capable in general of confusing *necessitas consequentiae* with *necessitas consequentis*, but it is absurd to diagnose this fallacy here.[3] It consists in a wrong shift of the necessity operator. Thus whoever commits it takes the operator to have the same meaning (though not scope) after the shift as before. The initial terms are not altered but rearranged. But Aristotle's error (if error it is) does not match this pattern. For merely by arranging the terms in (9) one could neither reach nor seem to reach the conclusion (1).

This is because the two modal propositions in (2), from which (9) follows, express principles which are taken to hold, and to hold necessarily, regardless of what the facts at t happen to be. This is apparent in the one case where Aristotle works out an application of the negative RT-condition in some detail, viz. in his *De Caelo* argument from 'always' to 'necessarily'. This argument has to be spurious, which is unfortunate for anyone trying to make sense of his rule for RT. But for the present I continue to assume the conclusion for which I shall argue in the next chapter, namely that the trick

[3] Cf. McCall, op. cit., p. 430.

can be explained in a way that exculpates RT. The point of interest now is that to obtain his result Aristotle resorts to universal principles. The proposition corresponding to 'r' is impossible in principle, for it is an outright self-contradiction, while the rules by which he imagines he can derive this 'r' from the proposition corresponding to '$(q/t$ & $Fp)$' are rules of logic. For the present discussion it is enough that the necessities to which he appeals in applying the RT-condition are law-like necessities, or principles, logical or non-logical, whose truth would not vary with the facts. Thus to take an uncontroversial case not used by Aristotle: one would reason to the result that it is impossible at t that X should enter the adolescent stage (being already mature at t) by alluding to the conceptual impossibility that any mature creature should grow up. No doubt the mutually exclusive concepts derive their force from our empirical knowledge of certain irreversible processes. But even so, the RT-condition rests on a law, in this case a law of nature.

Unless the modalities in the RT-condition expressed law-like necessity, how could Aristotle establish RT-results-on-a-hypothesis? For it is natural to assume that his method for determining whether 'p' *would* be possible at a time when q is merely *hypothesized* to obtain is exactly the same as his method for determining the categorical results, except that in the former case 'q/t' is unasserted. Thus the reasoning *actually* used (when the truth of 'q/t' is unknown) to support the result: ' "p" *would* be possible/impossible at t *if* q at t', is identical with the reasoning that *would* be used (if the truth of 'q/t' were known) to support: ' "p" *is* possible/impossible at t, *given* q at t'. But this identity presupposes that the necessities cited in the RT-condition are constant as between an actual situation at t, in which 'q' is false for all we know, and a hypothesized one in which it figures as true.

Now 'Nec$(q/t \supset \sim Fp)$' ((9) above), since it follows from the modal propositions in (2), expresses the same kind of necessity as they, i.e. lawlike necessity. And anyone who wrongly transferred the operator so as to produce '$q/t \supset$ Nec$(\sim Fp)$' would be attaching the same necessity to '$\sim Fp$'. Hence given that q/t, *modus ponens* yields the conclusion that it is a matter of lawlike necessity that not-Fp. This is the

meaning of (14) above. But then (14) implies that necessarily
not-Fp no matter what the facts, and in particular, no matter
whether 'q' is true or not at t. It is clear that this result,
which is the natural product of the fallacy suggested above
to explain the derivation of (1) from (2), is very different
from (1); for (1) is devoid of any implication that 'p', or for
that matter 'Fp', would have been impossible at t even if not
q then. There is therefore no reason to think that the RT rule
is founded on that fallacy.

Why should we suspect it of fallacy at all? Someone who
infers from (2) that '∼Fp' has the necessity of a law can be
easily brought to see that he is astray: we can point to plenty
of obvious examples where the premiss is true and the conclusion false. But if someone insists that (2) is grounds for
(1), where are the counter-examples to shake him? Intuitively
it seems that unless (1) is meaningless, it means something
that would have to be true precisely when (2) is.

All the same, it might be objected, a proposition asserting
necessity of whatever kind cannot follow from a conjunction
one of whose members is a merely factual proposition, i.e.
'q/t'. But this too can be answered, although to do so we
must use the RT rule itself in its own defence. So far it has
been seen as an instrument for deciding the modal status-at-t
of the undated 'p'. Let us now apply it to the dated 'q/t'
(where 'q' continues to serve as the description of the facts
at t). Given that q/t, the supposition that '∼q/t' should ever
be true entails a contradiction. Thus by the rule it is impossible at t that ∼q/t. This impossibility is of the same kind
as that asserted in (1). For there is no suggestion that '∼q/t'
would have been impossible at t no matter what, or, in particular, even if 'q' had been false at t. On the contrary, on
that hypothesis '∼q/t' would have been necessary at t, since
'q/t' would then have been impossible for just the reason
that '∼q/t' is in fact impossible then, and 'q/t' necessary.
Thus (2) entails 'Nec/t(q/t)' and 'Nec(q/t ⊃ ∼Fp)'. From
this pair of modal propositions we can respectably derive
'Nec/t(∼Fp)', or 'Imposs/t(Fp)'. One of the premisses asserts
lawlike necessity, the other a weaker kind, and the conclusion is no stronger than its weaker premiss.

So (2) entails 'Imposs/t(Fp)'. This is not quite the same as (1), which is 'Imposs/$t(p)$'. But the difference is negligible when 'p' is false at t (which is the circumstance under which we have to resort to the RT rule to decide whether it is possible). For in that case it is impossible at t that p/t. And if in addition it is impossible at t that Fp (i.e. that p at any later time), then from the standpoint of t there is *no* time to which the truth of 'p' can be referred consistently with the facts at t. (We may leave aside the question of its truth at earlier times, since the rule determines only what is possible from a given time forwards.[4]) Thus at t it is impossible that 'p' *simpliciter*, or, in other words: Imposs/$t(p)$.

However great Aristotle's anxiety to maintain and display the difference between the impossible and the false, he cannot (using RT) avoid their coincidence in the case where what is said to be false is a dated proposition, and its modality is assigned to that same date. In view of this paradoxical result it may be thought that he would not have sanctioned the application of the RT rule to dated propositions. After all, in *De Caelo* I.12 he is concerned only with such possibilities as 'X stands (*simpliciter*)', as opposed to 'X stands at such and such a time'. And his habit of verbally glossing over the difference between possibility in the formal sense and capacity[5] seems to reinforce this point. It does not make sense to speak of a capacity for standing-at-t, but only for standing. A man who is on his feet on repeated occasions exercises the same capacity many times, and on each occasion he continues exercising it for a length of time. But if there were a capacity for standing-at-t, it would be different from the capacity for standing-at-$t+n$. Hence every time the man was standing he would be realizing a different capacity. And each time he would, throughout the period of standing, exercise first the capacity for standing-at-t, then that for standing a moment later, then for a moment later, and so on as long as he maintained the position. Since the continuity of time entails that there is no such thing as *the* moment later than any given moment, there would be as indefinitely many capacities exercised in any finite stretch of standing as there are units into

---

[4] See above, pp. 28 ff.
[5] See above, ibid. and p. 33.

which the time can be divided.[6] Hence capacities make sense only if they are for states and activities *simpliciter*, not dated. And it might be supposed that this is how Aristotle views formal possibility too, in so far as he calls both this and capacity by the name of 'δύναμις'. Hence it might seem that for him the paradoxical equivalence of '~p/t' and 'Imposs/t (p/t)' cannot arise.[7]

On such a view we forfeit (anyway as far as Aristotle is concerned) the defence of RT suggested above. However Aristotle's language does not warrant this conclusion. For as well as 'δύνασθαι' he uses the term 'ἐνδέχεσθαι' to speak of possibility, and the latter has no special link with the idea of capacity that would weight its use in favour of possibilities for undated situations. And in *De Interpretatione* 9 he employs both terms in defending the contingency of 'There will be a sea-battle *tomorrow*'. The context makes it natural to take 'tomorrow' as having fixed reference; so what is at stake in this passage is the modal status of a proposition concerning the state of affairs at a given time.

But in any case the equivalence of '~p/t' with 'Imposs/t (p/t)' is no cause for alarm. It does not herald the general coincidence between truth and necessity that would do away altogether with contingent propositions. 'Imposs/t(p/t)' does not, for instance, entail the impossibility at t of 'p' *simpliciter*. This would follow only if it entailed 'Imposs/t ($p/t+1$) & Imposs/t($p/t+2$) & etc.' for every future time to which the truth of 'p' might be referred. But 'Imposs/t(p/t)' no more entails this than '~p/t' does, since they are logically equivalent. Both then are consistent with 'Poss/t(p) & Poss/t (~p)', i.e. with 'At t it is contingent whether or not p'. 'Imposs/t(p/t)' is also consistent with the prior contingency of 'p/t' itself. For from the fact that 'p/t' is impossible at t, given that '~p' is true then, it does not follow that there were not earlier times when it was not impossible that 'p/t'.[8]

---

[6] Since for Aristotle the temporal divisions are not actual unless someone in fact mentally divides the time, the number of real capacities for dated standing the man exercises would depend not on what he is doing but on how it is viewed.

[7] However he mentions it explicitly in *De Int.* 9. See below, pp. 89 f.

[8] In which case 'p/t' *was* contingent and *became* impossible. On change in modality through time cf. J.L. Ackrill, *Aristotle's 'Categories' and 'De Interpretatione'*, Oxford 1962, p.139; S.M. Cahn, *Fate, Logic and Time*, New Haven

Thus 'Imposs/$t(p/t)$' is consistent with 'Poss/$t'(p/t)$', where t' is earlier than t, and also of course with 'Poss/$t'(\sim p/t)$'. And since '$\sim p/t$' is equivalent to 'Imposs/$t(p/t)$', the latter too may be contingent in the same way: i.e. there may have been a time when it was possible that it would not be impossible at t that p at t.

'Nec/$t(p/t)$' is the weakest assertion of necessity that can be made in terms of dated modalities. It is consistent not only with its own prior contingency and with the prior possibility that $\sim p/t$, but also with the prior possibility of every similar proposition, '$\sim p/t+1$', '$\sim p/t+2$', '$\sim p/t+3$', etc. 'Nec/$t(p/t)$' is further consistent with the possibility at any and every time, including t, of the undated '$\sim p$'. The strongest assertion of necessity formulable in these terms would be a statement to the effect that there is never a time when the undated '$\sim p$' is possible, or, equivalently, that no dated proposition '$\sim p/t$', '$\sim p/t'$', '$\sim p/t''$', etc. is possible at any time prior to the date. On that assumption the necessity-at-t that p/t is not a necessity that was ever contingent: since it was always necessary in advance that p/t, it was always necessary in advance that Nec/$t(p/t)$.

In the earlier discussion of possibility- and impossibility-at-a-time, it was observed that the modality does not belong to the time as such, but to this considered as the locus of a state of affairs in virtue of which so and so is then possible/impossible. In the same way, we may say that to assert that it is in the strongest sense necessary that p is to assert that at all times the state of things is such as to exclude its ever becoming true that not-p. It is clear that necessity in this sense (which I shall call the strongest RT-sense, since it is spelt out in terms derived from the analysis of the RT rule) is weaker than logical necessity as we understand it. A logically necessary proposition is true in every logically possible situation, i.e. in any that can be described without self-contradiction. But there are logically possible situations in which what is in the strongest RT-sense necessary cannot be guaranteed true. E.g. it is logically possible that there should have existed a

1967, pp.129 ff.; R.C. Jeffrey, 'Coming True', in *Intention and Intentionality, Essays in Honour of G.E.M. Anscombe*, ed. C. Diamond and J. Teichman, Sussex 1979, pp. 251–260.

different system of nature, or none at all. But from the pro-position that things always *are* such as to exclude the falsity of '*p*' it does not follow that if the world had been entirely different '*p*' would still have been true.

This is not however a reason for saying that the strongest RT-necessity is not genuine necessity. Propositions necessary in this sense are true in all those situations that are in the corresponding sense possible: that is to say, in all those of which it can be said that at some time things are or have been such as not to exclude their later occurrence. For if '*q*' entailed the falsity of '*p*', and '*p*' were in the strongest RT-sense necessary, then the truth of '*q*' (ever) would be al-ways excluded, for any '*q*'.

We are now in a position to address the second question raised at the start of this chapter: what is the character of the necessity belonging to the principles employed in the RT-condition? I shall argue that as far as Aristotle is concerned, it must be construed as necessity of the strongest RT-type.

In the example worked out in *De Caelo* I.12, the principles are logically necessary. So far as this phrase means that they are necessarily true for reasons of logic, Aristotle might happily accept the description. But now the question is whether he also recognizes a distinct kind of necessity, the logical, as compared with RT-necessity. I assume that if so, he would recognize it as being stronger and in no way based on "the way things actually are". By implication he would also be committed to accepting logical possibility as more in-clusive than its RT-counterpart.

This is initially an attractive idea because it means that the RT rule *defines* the RT-modalities in other, though still modal, terms. It is true that in *De Caelo* he does not say that he is using the rule to define RT-possibility in other terms. But then there might not seem to him any need to say this. In any case he would have the material for a genuine defi-nition: one, incidentally, that defeats any theory that he was in general disposed to define modality by extensional con-cepts. For if he distinctly recognized the logical modalities, he can hardly be supposed to have thought *them* definable extensionally. (From this recognition it would not follow that when in *Prior Analytics* I.14, 33a25, he speaks of his

'ὁρισμός' of contingency, he means or has the right to mean a
definition in the strict sense. This would be so only if the
contingency spoken of there were RT-contingency.[9] If it is,
or includes, logical contingency, then the so-called ὁρισμός is,
as we saw before,[10] no genuine definition but only an explanation—of logical contingency in terms of logical necessity.)

Now in *De Caelo* I.11 Aristotle discusses different senses,
weaker and stronger, of 'imperishable'. At 280b31ff. he distinguishes the 'strictest' or 'primary' sense ('τὸ μάλιστα
κυρίως') as that which applies only to 'what is and has no
possibility of perishing, i.e. of being now and later not being,
or possibly later not being' (cf. 281a3-4). He is evidently
also employing 'impossible' here in the strictest sense he
knows, whatever that is. His list of the weaker senses of 'imperishable' certainly does not include one formed with the
strongest RT-concept of 'impossible'. Hence the latter may
be what he has in mind in the passage just quoted. Or he may
mean something stronger still. (The references to *now* and
later do not especially favour an RT-interpretation, since
they are implied by 'perishing' regardless of the kind of
perish*ability* that is being denied.)

The discussion in 11 is preparatory to the argument in 12,
where he purports to demonstrate in RT-terms that if X always is, there is no possibility of its not being, either through
ceasing or through having at some time not been. Part of this
conclusion, then, is the assertion that what always is, is imperishable. At 281b25 Aristotle announces this result as
follows: 'Whatever always is, is imperishable *simpliciter*
(ἁπλῶς).' No doubt *'simpliciter'* partly harks back to the
contrast drawn somewhat earlier with 'on-a-hypothesis'.[11]
In the light of that he is now saying: *given* that something
always is (and Aristotle does believe this to be given), then it
is, categorically, imperishable (not merely: would be so if
some further condition were fulfilled). But in this context
'simpliciter' (i.e. 'without qualification') also makes another
claim. It says that the imperishability Aristotle thinks he has

---

[9] The lack of any reference to time does not rule this out.
[10] See p. 16.
[11] See above, pp. 18-19; 32.

deduced from omnitemporal being is imperishability in the strongest and strictest sense. Even without a special verbal signal this is the only possible way of reading the conclusion of 12. Throughout the chapter the imperishability and ingenerability of omnitemporal being is declared without the slightest qualification and is starkly contrasted with the contingency of things that are and are not at different times. Hence what Aristotle thinks he has proved is that if X always is, it is in the strongest sense impossible that X should perish.

I say 'Aristotle thinks he has proved . . .', because he reaches the conclusion by means of the rule for RT, but, as I shall show in the next chapter, he would not be justified in this if he did not make certain dubious assumptions. For the moment, however, what matters is that this is in fact the rule by which he gets: 'If X always is, then it is impossible that X should perish'. Hence the 'impossible' in the consequent must be of the RT-type, making reference to the way things are at a time. If the antecedent is asserted, as by Aristotle it is, we have a categorical RT-result; otherwise we have what *would* be a categorical RT-result if the antecedent *were* asserted. It is clear too that this impossibility must be the strongest formulable in RT-terms. Thus the proposition 'X is imperishable' here means: 'At all times t, things are such that it is impossible at t that X should perish at any subsequent time'.

This then is the concept of impossibility which Aristotle has in mind when he speaks of the 'strict' (or 'primary') sense. That is: he does not merely view this as the strongest RT-type impossibility (though weaker than some other type), but as, quite simply, the strongest. But the necessity of the principles in the RT-condition must be at least as strong. Their necessity, then, consists in the fact that at all times t, things are such that it is impossible at t that these propositions should ever later be false.

But how can the necessity of the principles be only as strong as the impossibility that figures in the result? For let it be granted that if X always is, it is always impossible that X should not be, and granted also that X always is. It follows that X's not-being *is* always impossible: but not that it *would* have been even if the antecedent of the hypothetical had been false. In that case 'X is not' would have been true.

Whereas the sort of principles that Aristotle uses in his RT-condition, e.g. the principle of non-contradiction, would have been true whether or not X had always existed. There is this difference; but it does not entail that the necessity of the principles is stronger. That would be so only if a situation were *possible* in which 'not both p and not-p' is true and 'X is' false. But the facts being as they are, there is (in RT-terms) no possible situation in which X is not. We can assume that X is not (while knowing this to be in RT-terms wholly impossible) and still see what would follow from that assumption by the laws of logic. But our power to do this does not prove that the impossibility of the assumption is weaker than the necessity of the laws. For we can suppose even that $(p \& \sim p)$, and using logic reason that in that case p, and also $\sim p$, and so $(p \lor q)$, and also $(\sim p \lor q)$, and hence q (for any q), and so on. But in so doing we do not imply that the logical impossibility of '$(p \& \sim p)$' is weaker than the logical necessity of '$(p \& q) \supset p$', '$p \supset (p \lor q)$', etc.

It is true that not all negative RT-results involve impossibility as strong as the necessity of the principles. Thus it is impossible at t that X, then mature, should enter on adolescence; but the latter was not always impossible. The necessity of the principles is stronger because they were necessary even when X's adolescence was still contingent. But when the impossibility stated by the result is itself omnitemporal, there is no ground (or none formulable in RT-terms) for regarding this as less stringent than the principles. Hence the modality that figures in the RT-condition is in all cases of the same general kind (temporalized) as that appearing in the RT-results, and in some cases it is no stronger. It does not follow, however, that Aristotle is committed to holding that the principles themselves are arrived at only as RT-results. That would be absurd, since every application of the RT rule presupposes principles. Just as some truths, but not all, are known by means of others, so it is with omnitemporal necessities. But there is no more reason with necessity than with truth to ascribe to the derived and the underived a difference of kind or degree.

Aristotle is sometimes described as distinguishing between

'absolute' and 'relative' necessity.[12] 'Absolute' is used to translate 'ἁπλῶς', but the English word is misleading. By 'ἁπλῶς' he sometimes means 'categorically', sometimes 'omnitemporally',[13] and both are consistent with the relativization of necessity to the actual. *De Caelo*, moreover, suggests that all Aristotelian necessity is relative in this way. That is, it is never "absolute" in any sense implying total independence of fact. The statement that '*p*' is (categorically) omnitemporally necessary implies or presupposes the reality of this universe whose possible states and changes must conform to '*p*'.

The general point that an epistemological difference does not entail a difference in kind or degree of necessity is relevant when we consider that RT-terms allow no distinction between logical truths and laws of nature. If there are universally prevailing natural limits on the developments possible from actual situations, then anything which lies outside these is, in RT-terms, quite simply impossible, even if the description entails no self-contradiction. It may in some sense be conceivable, but (for anyone who knows it to be physically impossible) it is not conceivable that it *should be real.* From this point of view, physical necessity is not a special kind of necessity: it is the necessity of a certain kind of principle which differs from the logical kind in the way in which it is known. The necessity of a truth of logic is shown by proving the negation self-contradictory. This is an infallible criterion of necessity, but it is not what necessity consists in. For certain physical propositions share the same necessity, yet their negations entail no contradiction. It may even be granted that physical principles can never be known for certain (not that Aristotle preoccupies himself with this problem). What this means is that we can never be entirely confident that our efforts to identify natural laws have succeeded. But this does not affect the point. *If* there are omnitemporal natural necessities, then whatever they are, knowable or not,

---

[12] See e.g. W. & M. Kneale, pp. 92 ff.
[13] E.g. at *De Int.* 9, 19a26, as I understand it. See below, pp. 89 f.

they are no less binding than logic in the eyes of a philosopher who views modality only in RT-terms.[14]

The interpreter's task would be easier if in *De Caelo* Aristotle had stated that he is there using a "special" kind of modal concepts—dated and relative to actuality. His silence confirms the impression which the detail of the text has already been seen to support: that for him modality *is* RT-modality. Nor is this impression dispelled by his discussions elsewhere.[15] Although he does not follow Plato[16] so far as to contrast necessity with reason, he appears to have been unswayed by whatever considerations lead some philosophers to refuse to treat as strictly necessary anything not rationally intelligible. The necessary is the inevitable, what nothing can escape, and if the contents and workings of the natural order are not self-explanatory, this fact does not license thoughts of "other possible worlds". A "world" is not something whose existence is possible, since possibility and its opposite belong only within the world, being assigned to times in actual history. Hence it is not even correct to say that this world is the only one possible, since nothing is either possible or necessary except in relation to it. Aristotle's God, notoriously, is neither craftsman nor creator of the Universe. By his own logic of modality Aristotle was bound to adopt this position. Creation and craft imply choice to make one thing rather than another, or rather than nothing at all. But in RT-terms there is no choice where the "thing" is a world: this is not a *possible* alternative.

---

[14] At *Metaph*. K.8, 1064b32–4, speaking of what is 'omnitemporal and necessary', he says that the relevant sense of 'necessity' is not 'constraint', but 'that which we employ in demonstrations'. If I am right, he is referring as much to the necessity by which conclusions follow from premisses as to that of premisses and conclusions themselves.

[15] See below, pp. 83 ff.

[16] *Timaeus* 48.

'Always' and 'Necessarily' in *De Caelo* I.12

My argument so far has been that in *De Caelo* I.12 Aristotle operates from a conception of possibility as temporalized and relative to the actual. The passages cited support this interpretation, and the concept itself has appeared clear and coherent. It has proved capable of withstanding a logical objection to its use in categorical modal statements, and also of generating a sense of 'necessary' strong enough to characterize the laws of nature and of logic. But in reaching these results I deliberately set on one side the most salient fact about the text from which they were drawn. This is that Aristotle introduces his notion of 'possible' precisely in order to uphold the highly dubious conclusion: 'What always is, is (in the strongest sense) incapable of coming into being or passing away', or in other words: 'If so and so always is, it is (in the strongest sense) impossible that it should ever not be'. We have now to see how Aristotle's concept of possibility can provide even the appearance of support for this proposition, if that concept is as I have argued it to be.

From now on 'necessary' and 'impossible' will be used as meaning 'necessary/impossible in the strongest sense'. And 'always' here is also meant without restriction: i.e. not limited by a (possibly tacit) 'when. . .' clause (as in 'He always greets us politely'). 'It is impossible that not-p ever' says no more than 'It is impossible that not-p (or: necessary that p)'. Aristotle's conclusion, then, is B', the second of the problematic propositions from which this study began: 'If always p, then necessarily p'.

If 'necessary' is understood as 'logically necessary' in the modern sense (i.e. as meaning that the negation is self-contradictory), B' is obviously false, as is its fellow A' (= 'If it is possible that p, then at some time p'). In view of this, a common reaction to Aristotle's argument is the instant diagnosis of an illicit shift of 'necessarily' from its correct position in front of 'If always p, then p'. However, a reaction promising more interesting results would be to deduce that Aristotle is not employing the modern logical modalities. (In that case if he does make a mistake, it may not be such a crude one.) A study of the text, and especially of the key phrase 'at another time', has borne this out. However, the RT-modalities elicited by our analysis above give no better grounds for A' and B' than do their non-temporalized, non-relative counterparts. From the fact that the state of things at some time is such that a description of this together with the supposition that 'p' is later true entails no impossible consequence, it does not follow that 'p' ever will be or was true. And whereas in RT-terms 'always p' does entail a proposition asserting the necessity of 'p', this proposition is only: 'For every time t, it is necessary at t that p at t'. This is the universal generalization from: 'It is necessary at t that p at t', which by RT is logically equivalent to: 'p at t'. But 'For every time t it is necessary at t that p at t' says less than that 'p' is necessary in the strongest sense. For the latter means that for every time t, it is necessary at t that p *at all future times*.

Thus the concept earlier expounded of temporalized possibility is tied at one end to the actual world, viz. to the situation-relative-to-which that dates the modal operator. But it is free at the other, neither issuing in nor presupposing the truth of what is said to be possible. At t there may be the possibility that p and also the possibility that not-p, and although at all times, past, present and future, either 'p' is true or 'not-p' is, each of the possibilities-at-t is in itself logically consistent with its own total non-realization.

However, this holds good only on a proviso which so far I have taken for granted. This is that we refuse to regard the situation-relative-to-which as including in itself the prior truth of: 'It will be the case that p' or of its negation: 'It will never be the case that p'. If the first is included, the possibility-at-t of 'p' entails its own realization, and if the second, then 'p' is impossible at t. Hence if as a matter of fact 'p' is always false, and if "the facts" at any and every time are taken to include the future truth for ever of 'not-p', then at all times things are such as to exclude its ever becoming true that '*p*', and '*p*' will be impossible in the strongest sense, and 'not-*p*' necessary.

Now it may be thought that Aristotle reaches his *De Caelo* I.12 conclusion by ignoring or cancelling the proviso. His argument would be not only plausible but in RT-terms valid on this interpretation. But the text does not warrant it. There is no sign that he has present truths about the future in mind at all here. The situation-relative-to-which the man is said to have the possibility of standing is described simply as that in which he is sitting: not as that in which he is sitting and also has it true of him that he will be standing. However, the hypothesis may seem to be indirectly confirmed by *De Interpretatione* 9, which is concerned with the relation between the prior truth and falsity of future-tensed statements and the necessity or contingency of the events those statements are about. Many have thought that Aristotle's conclusion there is that some future-tensed statements must be regarded as neither true nor false in advance, since otherwise nothing would count as contingent (a consequence he takes to be absurd). *If* this is his argument (which is by no means certain) its rationale *may* be the consideration that advance truth would have to be included in the prior situation-relative-to-which, so that if it is now true that something will never happen, its happening is now impossible. Perhaps Aristotle thought that the only or the safest way to avoid inclusion was to deny prior truth-values outright. It is in this chapter that he speaks of the cloak that can but never will be cut up;[1] and perhaps for the reason just mentioned he sees this as failing to make sense unless prior truth-value is denied. If this account of *De Interpretatione* 9 were acceptable, we should have some ground for supposing the same idea at work in *De Caelo* I.12, despite the absence of local evidence. Only here it would operate in reverse. That is: in *De Caelo* I.12 Aristotle takes for granted prior truth-value, and argues from this to the impossibility that something should ever not be, given that it always will be.

But this is not at all plausible, because even if the logic of the two passages is the same, and is as suggested, the end-results are (on this view) directly opposed. In *De Caelo* I.12

[1] 19a12-15.

Aristotle aims finally at the categorical conclusion that certain things cannot not be (it being taken as given that they always are). And those statements in *De Interpretatione* 9 that are commonly read as denials of prior truth-value are undisputably categorical. Thus in the latter work he allegedly rejects (at least for a certain class of cases) the proposition allegedly required for the conclusion of the former. So the conclusion of *De Interpretatione* 9 would contradict a premiss of *De Caelo* I.12. The arguments subvert each other if they proceed on the principle suggested. We should expect some sign, locally or elsewhere, that Aristotle was not always unshakenly assured of both results. There are no indications of this, and both seem to be carried forward to later works. For instance, whatever the nature of his defence of contingency in *De Interpretatione* 9, he seems in *Nicomachean Ethics* III[2] to be still quite sure that nothing has arisen to overturn it. *Metaphysics* Θ.8, 1050b6ff. stands in a similar relation to the upshot of *De Caelo* I.12. Moreover there is some evidence that he went over parts of *De Caelo* after composing them, relating them to passages in subsequent writings commonly held to postdate *De Interpretatione*. If he had the opportunity to reconsider but did not take it, the reasonable conclusion must be that he detected no discrepancy between the two earlier positions, although the conflict must have been obvious had they been reached in the manner suggested.

Later I shall argue that in fact the concept of truth-in-advance is not what is at stake in *De Interpretatione* 9,[3] or at least not in a way that could sustain a direct inference from 'always' to 'necessarily' so as to explain *De Caelo* I.12. The one attraction of the proposal just rejected is that taken in conjunction with the RT-modalities it gives Aristotle a valid argument for propositions A′ and B′. However, this is beside the point unless it is already fairly certain that Aristotle's modalities *are* the RT-ones—a position which we

---

[2] Deliberation is rational only if the subject matter is rationally assumed to be contingent. In III.3 where Aristotle explains this (cf. *De Int.* 9, 18b31ff.) he evidently holds that deliberation *is* in some cases rational.

[3] See below, Chapter V and pp. 141 ff.

cannot treat as fully established without first showing how these concepts might have generated A' and B'.

It may be suggested that he does commit the error of which he is often accused in this context, namely a faulty operator-shift—only in RT-terms rather than in terms of absolute modality. Thus he could have reached B' by going from 'It is always necessary that it should always be the case that if always p then p' to 'If always p then it is always necessary that always p'. But this is unlikely in view of the fact that in *De Caelo* I.12, 281b9 ff., a few lines before B' is announced as proved, Aristotle is very concerned to remind us that the total impossibility of simultaneous sitting and standing does not entail that the sitting man has no possibility of standing. Such nearby concern about the correct positioning of the strong modal operator does not encourage us to attribute B' to a mistake on precisely that point.

Hintikka too is reluctant to accept that B' originates in a logical fallacy of this type[4] (although he does not observe that in Aristotle's case the fallacy would have been perpetrated, if at all, in terms of strong RT-impossibility rather than our own absolute counterpart). Hintikka traces A' and B' to a source in deep confusion affecting Aristotle's entire approach to modality. He focusses, in the first place, on Aristotle's method of deciding possibility by supposing-true-at-another-time. In Hintikka's view, Aristotle cannot see how to frame such a supposition without committing himself to the truth of what is supposed. The result is that as soon as he uses his rule for applying 'possibly not-p', before ever getting so far as to consider whether 'an absurd consequence follows', he has already by the act of supposition assumed that 'not-p' represents a fact. It follows that if for some reason he believes that 'not-p' is always false, he cannot even begin to consider the question of its possibility, and so must treat it as impossible. Thus although perhaps he does not officially think of 'possibly' as meaning the same as 'at some time', he consistently mishandles its rule of use in a way that gives the same logical results as a formal statement of synonymy.

This suggestion would be very implausible if it were simply that Aristotle cannot distinguish between hypothesis and assertion. Nothing could be clearer than the contrast he draws between 'categorical' and 'on-a-hypothesis' in *De Caelo* I.12 and frequently elsewhere. But Hintikka thinks that it is not hypothesis as such that Aristotle conflates with assertion, but hypothesizing the truth of '*p*' (or 'not-*p*') *at a time*. For any time referred to, whether definitely or indefinitely, will be a time in the actual history of the world. And Hintikka sees that for Aristotle there are no other possible worlds with their own temporal orders whose moments stand in no temporal relations to the events of actual history. In Hintikka's phrase, the time to which the supposed truth is referred is an 'actual now' (p.212). Thus he speaks of Aristotle as assuming:

that every moment of time during any course of events that we consider possible must be equated with some moment of time during the actual course of events. This must have seemed a very natural assumption, for how could there be moments of time not identical with some moment of time in the actual history of the universe? (p.208.)

But why should this lead to a merging of supposition with assertion? Hintikka's language is not very clear, but his idea seems to be this: in thinking of a time as a time in actual history, Aristotle identifies it as the locus of whatever events he believes actually do occur in it. Hence if he believes that *p* will be the case at *t*, the sentence 'not-*p* at *t*' is not merely false, but for him inconsistent. And this is so even if this sentence is used only to put forward a supposition. Hence he cannot coherently make a time-referring supposition without believing it to be true. Thus if he thinks that '*p*' is always false, he cannot regard it as possible, since this would involve the incoherent supposition that '*p*' is true at a time which, being a time of actual events, is, and is identified as, a time when '*p*' is false. This seems to be the reasoning behind Hintikka's description of Aristotle as:

motivated by the idea that the only way we can think of a possibility to be realized is at some moment of time in our 'actual history of the world'. But if other things than those assumed actually take place at that moment, a contradiction does seem to result. (p.109.)

And similarly:

If Aristotle's definition [*sc.* of possibility in terms of supposing] is combined with the assumption that possibilities can be assumed to be realized only within this gradually unfolding progression of actual nows, it leads straight to the principle of plenitude [Hintikka's label for proposition A']. (p. 212.)

If this is what lies behind A' and B', then Aristotle is indeed confused. His own doctrine of time does not warrant the position ascribed by Hintikka. It is true that he does not regard time or times as having reality independently of actual change in actual substances. But this does not entail that he cannot coherently suppose an event not to happen at a time when he knows it does. It is not as though the time can only be identified as the time of that event. Its status as "an actual now", i.e. as a moment in actual history, rests on the fact that *whatever* happens then, whether E_1 or some alternative E_2, is seen as occupying the same position *vis-à-vis* already actual events. It is not necessary to treat whichever event does happen as if it were an essential feature of its time, so that the time cannot be thought of as a time when something else might have happened. Nor is this entailed by Aristotle's concept of possibility, if this is the RT-concept analysed earlier. An RT-possible event E_1, should it occur, would be subsequent to some stretch (indefinitely long) of actual history. The same stretch would also have preceded an alternative event E_2, should E_2 occur instead of E_1. The position of E_1 (supposing this to be realized) can be defined by reference to actual past events, and it is this same position, thus defined, that E_2 would have filled had it happened instead. Thus the time of the possible event is 'identical with some moment of time in the actual history of the universe': but not in a way that entails that only the actual event was possible.

However, it is not Hintikka's thesis that Aristotle has sound reasons for the position alleged, nor even that he is always altogether happy with its consequences.[5] Proposition B' suits the cosmological purpose of *De Caelo*, but what of *De Interpretatione* 9, and the coat which can but never will be cut up? Hintikka has to reconcile this with B', since it is his view that in both works Aristotle's fundamental position is the same. He suggests that the possibility that this coat be cut up rests on the general possibility that such things should

---

[5] See above, pp. 13-14.

happen, which general possibility entails its own realization
in some instance though not in any particular one. But this
does not fit well with Hintikka's account of the basic confusion, nor with the form that B' takes in *De Caelo*. For why
should the alleged confusion operate on the generalized
supposition 'Something coat-like is at some time physically
divided' so as to generate automatically the corresponding
assertion, but leave the singular one unaffected? And in any
case, the text of *De Caelo* I.12 puts it beyond doubt that
Aristotle is there concerned with possibilities regarding individuals considered as such. Thus his conclusion is not: 'If a
type of situation S is always instantiated, then necessarily it
is instantiated', where the antecedent does not entail that any
one particular object is always or necessarily in the condition
of realizing S. Rather it is: 'If it is always the case that some
particular object is (or: is F), then it is necessarily the case
that that object is (or: is F)'.[6] And he equally clearly subscribes here to a proposition which entails a corresponding
version of A', i.e.: 'If it is possible that an object is and is
not, at different times, then *that* object is and is not, at
different times'.

There is no good independent evidence for Hintikka's
hypothesis of confusion over 'supposing "*p*" true at another
time'. The same goes for the other explanations of A' and B'
touched on so far. They are alike, too, in that all trace these
troublesome propositions to Aristotle's logical handling of
modal concepts. Either he applies them taking truth about
the future into account; or he makes an error in application
(e.g. a faulty operator-shift); or he radically misinterprets his
own rule of use (Hintikka). On each view Aristotle emerges
as holding or compelled to operate as if he holds A' and B' as
analytic propositions, true by reason only of the logic (or
pseudo-logic) governing the use of the modal and temporal
terms involved. Perhaps it is not surprising that attempts to
account for his position should focus on the logic of 'possible'
and allied terms. For in *De Caelo* I.12 Aristotle himself
moves straight from his explanation of the logical rule, with

---

[6] See e.g. 281b32, 'τὸ αὐτὸ καὶ ἕν'. Cf. C.J.F. Williams' detailed examination
of the logic of *De Caelo* I.12, 'Aristotle and Corruptibility', *Religious Studies* I
1965, pp. 95–107; 203–215. See esp. pp. 211–12.

its inbuilt reference to 'another time', to the questionable demonstration of B'. However, I shall now argue that in *De Caelo* B' and A' have a different basis, the evidence for which is firmly sited in the text. On the account to be given the Aristotelian concept of possibility is not irrelevant to these conclusions, but they depend also on premises of a non-formal nature. It will also emerge that the trick of the argument lies in these, not in Aristotle's modal concepts, nor in his use of them.

We must go back to *De Caelo* I.11, where Aristotle's discussion of possibility begins. He opens with some remarks about possibilities for maximal exercise. Here he equates 'possibility' with 'capacity', and we shall often find the latter term more convenient in the subsequent discussion.

Now if something has the possibility (δύναται) of motion[7] or lifting a weight, we always refer this to the maximum, as for instance lifting a hundred talents or walking a hundred stades. Although the subject can perform fractional tasks lying within the maximal limit (since it can also exceed these fractions) it is correct to define a possibility [or: capacity] by reference to the full amount and that which exceeds all others (πρὸς τὸ τέλος καὶ τὴν ὑπεροχὴν). So whatever can perform a maximum of so much must also be able to perform what lies within the maximum. For instance, if something can lift a hundred talents it can also lift two, and if it can walk a hundred stades, then also two. But the capacity is for the maximum. And if, referring to a maximum, we say that it is incapable of so much, then it is also incapable of greater amounts. For instance, the man who cannot walk a thousand stades clearly cannot walk a thousand and one. There is no difficulty about this. Let it be taken as settled that when 'capacity' is meant in the strict [or: primary] sense, it is defined by reference to the maximal limit (κατὰ τῆς ὑπεροχῆς τὸ τέλος). Someone may object that this is not necessarily so, since the man who sees a stade will not also see all the magnitudes contained in it: on the contrary, the one who can see a dot or hear a minute sound will have the perception of the greater ones too. But this does not affect our account. For the maximum is to be determined either in terms of the capacity or in terms of the object. What we say is clear. Superior vision has a smaller object, while superior speed covers a greater distance. (281a7–27.)

Why does Aristotle say that capacity in the strict (or primary) sense is to be defined by reference to a maximum? Not

---

[7] On the text cf. J.L. Stocks, Oxford translation ad loc.

all capacities are for maximizable exercises: e.g. the capacity to die. But at any rate he is clear that in those cases where a maximum is relevant, the full specification of the capacity would refer to it and not merely to the kind of effect. So a capacity to lift a hundred pounds, if this is the full specification, is a different one from the capacity to lift two hundred. It follows too that the capacity for the maximum is exercised even on those occasions when less than the full task is performed. If a man who can lift two hundred pounds lifts twenty, we must not say strictly speaking that he exercises a capacity for lifting twenty, since that would imply that beyond twenty he is unable to lift. It also follows that agents with different maxima are exercising different lifting capacities even if they lift the same actual weight.

After anchoring his account to homely examples of actions like walking and lifting, Aristotle applies it to *being* and *not being*. By 'being' he means being F where 'F' comes under one of his categories: being a certain type of substance, being white, being six foot high, etc. He says that the capacity for being F must also be specified by reference to a maximum, and in this case it is temporal. X has a greater capacity for being F than Y if it can be F for longer. And for anything that is F, there is a time longer than which it cannot be F. Presumably the particular period depends on the nature of the object.[8] In Aristotle's own words:

If then there are some things capable both of being and of not being, there must be a determinate time that is the maximum both of being and of not being; that is to say, a determinate time for the being, and for the not being, of which the object is capable.[9] 'Being' here may be in any category: e.g. being a man, or white, or three cubits long, etc. (12, 281a28–33.)

This passage occurs at the very beginning of chapter 12. During the ensuing discussion of being and possibility Aristotle omits to spell out 'being'/'not being' as meaning 'being F'/not being F' for some category of 'F'.[10] Thus he speaks of

[8] Cf. *De Gen. et Corr.* II.10, 336b9–15.
[9] The Greek here could also be translated: 'a determinate time during which the object is capable of being . . .', but the analogy with walking etc. shows that this is beside the point.
[10] Cf. *Metaph.* Θ.8, 1050b12–16.

things that 'always are', and things that 'sometimes are and sometimes are not'. Because of this it has often been assumed[11] that 'is' and 'is not' are existential in the body of the chapter. But since the argument depends on the opening lines just quoted, the 'is' of predication must be understood throughout (with the place of 'F' left blank for the sake of generality). And since throughout Aristotle treats 'X is' and 'X is not' as contradictories, he must be taking 'X is not F' as the contradictory of 'X is F'. The latter's external and internal negations are here equivalent. It is also possible to distinguish two internal negations: i.e. 'X is (not-F)' and 'X (not-is F)'. Aristotle treats these too as equivalent. Hence the conclusion (B′) for which he is aiming is: 'If something is always F (for an "F" in one of the categories) it is impossible that it should not be F (or: be not-F)'. Where 'F' is in a category other than Substance, the subject term of 'X is F' designates a concrete individual. Where the category is Substance, 'X' could be taken as designating either the individual (as in 'Socrates is a man') or the matter. Aristotle's argument requires the second alternative, for a reason which will become clear.

Meanwhile we can now see why, when discussing the initial examples of walking etc., he said that possibility or capacity in the strictest or primary sense must have included in its specification a reference to the maximum. Those illustrations preface a discussion not of capacity in general, but of those capacities whose content is given by a predicate in one of the Aristotelian categories. For a subject to be at all is, primarily, for it to be F for some set of these values of 'F'. There may be other things true of it, e.g. that it changes. But there is no category of change: change is from one categorizable property to another in the same category. In general all other true predications presuppose true predications from the categories. Thus the corresponding capacities are the logically primary capacities, since they are for the logically primary actualities. And Aristotle is saying that these actualities are for definite periods of exercise, and that

[11] E.g. by Guthrie and Stocks in their translations (Loeb and Oxford respectively).

references to the maxima should appear in proper specifications of the capacities.

In the passage last quoted, *not being* (i.e. not being F or being not-F) figures as something for which there is a capacity. This is introduced in tandem with the capacity for *being*: Aristotle first mentions them in connection with objects that have both. Capacities for negative conditions were already implied in the original examples. If someone's capacity for walking is for walking only so far, he cannot walk for ever, hence has, and sometimes "exercises", the capacity for not walking. By assigning to the positive condition a (finite) temporal maximum, Aristotle ensures that whatever has the capacity for this has also the capacity for the negative.

Thus in *De Caelo* I.12 both 'being' and 'not being' represent exercises of capacities. That is why 'X is' and 'X is not' cannot be interpreted existentially: it is nonsense to say that something non-existent is exercising a capacity (which presumably, therefore, *it has*) for non-existence. For the same reason, where 'F' is in the category of Substance, 'X' in 'X is not F' must designate the matter of, say, some deceased or as yet unformed concrete F-type substance. 'Socrates is not (any longer) a man' entails the present non-existence of the individual Socrates, though not of his matter. Hence if 'X is not a man' means 'X is exercising the capacity for not being a man', 'X' cannot be used as a name for Socrates or any individual man, since in that case the sentence has the absurd implication that a non-existent individual is exercising a capacity—a capacity, moreover, for not being what it is essential to him to be.

In a few sentences Aristotle moves a long way on the strength of the analogy with obvious maximum-related capacities such as the ability to lift weights. First he extends this to 'being F' for all 'F', and makes the maximum temporal. Secondly he assumes capacities for privations as well as positive conditions. And thirdly, as the text last quoted makes perfectly plain, he treats the capacity *for not being F* as no less maximum-related than its positive counterpart. Both have cut-off points for the exercise. Hence anything that has both will eventually cease to exercise whichever it happens to be exercising and begin to exercise the other. Given, then, that (a) '*p*' and 'not-*p*' are sentences affirming and denying some categorizable property of a subject; and (b) 'It is possible that *p*/not-*p*' is interpreted as saying that the subject has the capacity for the condition (whether positive or negative): we now have the premisses for a valid inference to A': 'If it is possible that *p*, then *p* at some time'.[12] For if it is possible that *p*, then not-*p* at some time; but if not-*p* at some time, then it is possible that not-*p*; and if it is possible that not-*p*, then *p* at some time.

So it is not Aristotle's logical rule for testing possibility by means of supposition that generates A'. On the present showing, he has mustered all the materials for concluding to A' before he even alludes to the rule. The last quotation takes us to 12, 281a33, and the rule is not mentioned until 281b 14-15.

A' in *De Caelo* I.12 has limited scope. The assumptions from which it follows are postulated only for predicates under the categories. Aristotle does not imply that the corresponding possibilities and capacities are the only ones. Hence he does not imply that there might not be possibilities for which A' does not hold: for instance, the never cut-up coat of *De Interpretatione* 9. The capacity for being cut up is not for a mode of categorizable *being*, but for a sort of change or ceasing. A' itself presupposes such capacities, but they do not fall under it. Granted that some state has an inherent span, it does not follow that it must pass away in just one way rather than another,[13] and some possibilities of ceasing will inevitably be unfulfilled for any given object. Nor is there any logical reason why they should be realized in other cases of the same kind.[14]

[12] See especially 282a10-12.

[13] Cf. *Top*.II.11, 115b17-18 and *Metaph*. E 3, 1027b8-11.

[14] R. Sorabji (*Necessity, Cause and Blame, Perspectives on Aristotle's Theory*, London, 1980, pp. 128-32) holds that A' applies only to everlasting subjects. This restriction is a consequence of our account, since A' entails eternal alternation between being F and not-F. But Aristotle does not say that the eternity as such of a subject brings it under A'. The connection depends on the idea of temporal maxima for states of *being*. However, even on this basis (with its implication that modes of becoming and ceasing do not fall under A') the reconciliation of *De Caelo* I.12 and *De Int*. 9 is not entirely straightforward. For at *Cat*. 4, 1b25 ff. (cf. 9, 11b1 ff.) πάσχειν is said to be a category, and is illustrated by 'being cut' (I owe this point to Jonathan Barnes). And although at *De Caelo* I.12, 281a30-33

Aristotle passes on to discuss the difference between the false and the impossible and the rule for detecting it. Any proposition can be true or false: it does not have to be a predication in one of the categories. When 'possible' and 'impossible' are, as here, lined up with 'true' and 'false', it is clear that they too are intended to be applicable to any type of case. Thus it is no surprise that they apply to cases for which A′ does not hold. (Not that Aristotle mentions this, or cites any such instances in this context. His examples of 'sitting' and 'standing' come under the category of Position. But he is concerned to prove B′, whose range is logically the same as that of A′, and it would not have seemed to him helpful to divert attention from the relevant area.)

In fact, the method of supposition in itself would be equally effective even if *no* propositions were recognized as satisfying the assumptions necessary for A′. Its use does not presuppose Aristotle's theory of primary (categorizable) being, nor his doctrine of temporal spans. No doubt we are right to suspect the credentials of A′. But the credentials of his formal rule for 'possible' are independent.

Aristotle begins I.12, then, by addressing himself to certain primary possibilities which he characterizes by reference to the *metaphysical* concept of temporal maxima. He then

---

Aristotle specifically mentions only Substance, Quality and Quantity, at 283a6–7 he says that the principle of temporal maxima applies to ποιεῖν and πάσχειν (see below, p. 70). But this is not a decisive objection to the reconciliation proposed above, because Aristotle seems to have different views on the status of πάσχειν. At *Physics* III.3 he equates κίνησις with ποιεῖν/πάσχειν, having first defined κίνησις (which here = becoming in general) in such a way that it cannot count as a category of being. The same would seem to follow for πάσχειν (although the issue is complicated by the apparently inconsequential appearance of this concept at III.1, 200b30; for a detailed discussion see S. Waterlow, *Nature, Change, and Agency in Aristotle's 'Physics'*, Oxford, 1982, Ch. III, Pt. I). If πάσχειν is κίνησις (seen from a certain point of view), then on *De Caelo* principles the unrealized possibility of being cut up does not infringe A′. But what of *De Caelo* 283a6–7, where πάσχειν is said to have determinate duration? This, I suggest, need not be taken to imply that Aristotle here thinks of it as a category of being (so that every case of πάσχειν ought to be covered by A′). The point may only be that where there is a continuous suffering of a certain affection (itself a state of being), as when something is not only made to be F, but kept F, then the suffering (and the agent's action) is limited to the intrinsic duration of the F-state. This does not apply to those sufferings that occur when something is made to begin or cease to be F.

moves to the more comprehensive *logic* by which these and all other possibilities are tested. But the difference in orientation of these two stages should not lead us to overlook their unity. It is not only that both are necessary steps to B'. There is also a common underlying theme of *change*. This concept lies at the basis of the method of supposing what is now false to be true at another time. And the idea of properties as having intrinsic maximum durations is essential to the metaphysical theory of change in a universe of Aristotelian substances.

For how can anything change unless for a reason? And what reason would there be if a thing could continue indefinitely in whatever state it happens to be in? If it could, that alone would prove the state not to be one of disequilibrium: so why change to another if the thing has already found its level? Of course some changes are due to interference from without. When this happens the change can be explained without postulating some kind of inherent temporal limit for the previous state. But for Aristotle change from without is secondary. Nothing could be changed in this way if it and other things did not also change "of themselves". Substances express their natures in patterns of unforced behaviour. Although liable to interference, there would be nothing to *be* interfered with if their activity were not already informed by its own internally regulated direction. The paradigm substances are living things.[15] And just as the size of the organism depends on its nature, not merely on external pressures, so with the duration of life itself and its phases. There are natural developments and cycles which pass through various stages. Each stage must have its proper temporal span. For if any were such as to continue of itself indefinitely, the process as a whole would be blocked: and blocked from *within* the system, which is as much as to say that the organism would from within itself be stifling its own most natural mode of existence. If Aristotle had taken the Newtonian particle as his model for physical substance, then even using his temporalized formal concept of possibility he would never have arrived at A'. Familiar maximum-related

---

[15] *Metaph.* Z.7, 1032a15-20.

capacities such as for weight-lifting would have seemed of no special significance: there would have been no *a priori* ground for assimilating 'time lasted' to 'weight lifted', let alone for making this the model for the primary type of possibility.

Thus at the centre of Aristotle's suppositional method lies 'change' for reasons of logic, and at the centre of this his metaphysics has placed the concept of natural temporal spans. But even with this metaphysical backing his passage to A' in *De Caelo* is not easy. To get the conclusion in a general form he has to wring from the concept of natural spans an abstract symmetry of function which its analogical basis cannot justify. His argument requires the assumption that the capacity for being in a negative condition is of the same kind of temporal structure as its positive counterpart, so that in both the condition is intrinsically timed. If only positive conditions had natural spans, then the possibility (capacity) for being not-F would entail its own realization at some time, but the possibility for being F would not. For something could have this possibility, yet go on indefinitely being not-F. But what can it mean to say that a negative condition, the absence of something, is inherently limited? The analogy with weight-lifting cannot begin to put life into this idea: on the contrary. What could be the maximum an agent is capable of not-lifting? Is it the greatest amount beyond what he *can* lift—i.e. the weight of all the heavy material in the Aristotelian universe? Is it the most he can *choose* not to lift, i.e. the most he can lift? Or is it the most he can not-lift the least he can lift? In that case there is no maximum, unless we say that the least is nothing at all. What would be the fractions falling within the limit (cf. 11, 281a 12–14)? Not-lifting a smaller weight includes not-lifting all greater ones, so perhaps the all-inclusive maximum is "the least weight". But if (since there is no "least") it is zero, the comparable temporal maximum for 'being not-F' would be: 'being F for no length of time at all'. But this suggests that the maximal exercise of being not-F would never give way, as A' requires, to its contradictory. And what sense can be made in teleological terms of the idea of an inbuilt *terminus* to a negative condition? It may be that for a healthy person there is a limit to the amount of time he can remain sitting, but why to the amount he can remain not sitting? Not-sitting gets its character, hence its duration, from whatever positively goes on in it: the positive contraries to sitting may each be intrinsically timed, but for not-sitting to have a regular span, it would be necessary that sitting recur always after a definite period. To fit Aristotle's specifications, not only must all possibilities of being F be for states with temporal maxima, but all must be for regularly recurring states like night and day and the seasons. Perhaps, however, we should charitably take him to be concerned with these not as the only cases, but as the ones central in his physics and cosmology. A' then would not be a universal principle for all predicates in the categories, but at best a limited truth about fundamental natural processes.[16]

Do the assumptions behind A' give adequate grounds for B'? Prima facie it seems not. If something is always F, then its capacity for being F is not limited. Hence it cannot cease being F on account of an inherent term. But it does not follow that it has no possibility at all of ceasing. There may be other possible causes, say external hindrance. But Aristotle finds no difficulty. Taking 'for an infinite time' as tantamount to 'always'[17] he argues that whatever is F for an infinite time cannot ever not be F, since this would imply that its exercise of being F is replaced eventually by an exercise of the opposite. But since, *ex hypothesi*, its being F lasts for an infinite time, there would have then to be a time beyond infinite time for the opposite condition to occupy. But an infinite time, he says (281a33–4), is a time greater than any that might be specified and lesser than none. Hence there is no time beyond infinite time, and infinite time is all time. So whatever is always F cannot not be so. For the truth of the supposition of its being not-F cannot be referred to a time beyond the time during which its F-ness is given. Hence that supposition, to be true, would have to be true at a time when its falsity is assumed as given; and so the supposition (relative to this given) is absurd (281b18ff.).

[16] However in *De Caelo* Aristotle does propose A' and B' universally: see 10, 280a32–4 and 12, 283b17–18.

[17] See below p. 69.

I shall say no more about the suggestion[18] that the sequence of thought here depends on confusing *necessitas consequentiae* with *consequentis* in connection with the truism 'If X is always F, then X is F'; but turn instead to another elementary fallacy which might be thought operative. This is the confusion of the collective and distributive uses of 'all'. Given that it is always false that X is not-F, if we try to suppose this true *at a time other than all the times* that figure in "the given", the supposition would indeed be absurd. It is not of course logically impossible (self-contradictory) that X is not-F, but it is impossible relative to the actual facts taken as a single block "given" in this way. Aristotle, I have argued, recognizes no sense of 'impossible' etc. that is not relativized to the actual, and in this system there are some (strongest) impossibilities that are not self-contradictory propositions. Hence if he reaches B' by wrongly taking 'all times' in the collective sense, his result is of the same general form as results that can be validly reached by RT-logic. Perhaps for this reason he is easily deceived. The obvious failure of 'X is not-F' to be a self-contradiction does not warn him that something has gone wrong, since there are sound arguments of the same stamp in which internally consistent propositions are shown to be impossible relative to some given. For instance, suppose we hold '*p*' to be a fundamental natural law, and take it to entail the non-tautology '*q*'. Given these premisses, it is at all times impossible that not-*q* ever. However, here the given includes the (presumed) fact that '*p*' is a law and is therefore itself necessary at all times. But if (as for Aristotle in his argument for B') the given is only given as *omnitemporal* and not as omnitemporally *necessary*, how can it follow that it or its consequences are anything more than merely omnitemporal?

There may all the same be the illusion of proof if 'all times' is used collectively. To invoke this illusion we have to curb the impulse to dismiss in advance as spurious any notion of time as a totality. (We shall see presently that in *De Caelo* I.12 Aristotle does in fact use this, in a way that makes a

---

[18] Endorsed e.g. by Williams, pp. 98 ff., who classifies the fallacy as one of division.

certain sense in the context of his metaphysics.) Now given collectively that X is F always, it does follow that it is impossible (in relation to this) that X should ever be not-F, if possibility consists merely in possible realization at some time. However, this is not the conclusion that Aristotle ought to be pursuing if he is using modal concepts in the way expounded in the last two chapters. For on that account a correct use involves a double temporal reference: as well as the time to which the supposition is referred, there is the time of the modality itself. Hence we are entitled to ask: given (collectively) that X is always F, *when* is 'X is not-F' impossible? The answer, as in other cases, is of course: when the given is given. But in this case the whole given will have been given only "at the end of time"; and *"then"* there is no time when the alleged impossibility can hold. The impossibility can be accepted as genuine (if we ignore doubts concerning the collectivization of 'always') only if it is regarded as timeless, which presupposes a scheme in which modality in general is timeless. Thus in RT-terms the proposition 'It is impossible that X is not-F' is incoherent if derived by taking 'always' collectively. Moreover, even if it were not absurd to postulate a time when time is over at which the impossibility holds, this would still not be what Aristotle wants, if our earlier analysis was correct. For according to that, to say that 'not-*p*' is impossible in the strongest sense is to say that its falsity (ever) is impossible at *t* for *every* *t*: not that it is impossible at some pseudo-time which, if it existed, would only be *one* time (and late at that). The impossibility of 'not-*p*' *"then"* is no guarantee that 'not-*p*' was *always* (i.e. at every genuine time) impossible.

However, the reason that makes it absurd to say that *when* time is over, *then* something is impossible, also makes it absurd to say that *then* the thing is possible. And it is the same whether we put '*p*' or 'not-*p*' for what is absurdly called 'possible then'. Perhaps Aristotle attended to some of these facts and ignored others. Thus we may conjecture that in relation to the collective given 'It is always the case that *p*', he focussed on the absurdity of saying: 'The given having been given, it is *then* possible that not-*p*'. This is absurd because 'then' refers to a pseudo-time which is really no time at all. Perceiving this, Aristotle might have thought that the best way to emend the above statement would be to write 'at no time' (= 'at a non-existent time') for 'then'. Thus he would have: 'Given (collectively) that p always, it is at *no time* possible that not-p'. And now it seems that he can draw the aimed-for conclusion B' simply by the standard transformation of 'at no time . . .' into 'at every time not. . .'. This yields him: 'Given (collectively) that p always, for every t it is impossible at t that not-p (ever)'; and now the phrases 'for every t' and 'ever' refer to genuine times falling within the time when 'p' is true. (The trick consists in first using 'at no time' as if (absurdly) it specified a non-existent but nonetheless identifiable *date at which* the possibility of 'not-p' obtains, and then returning the phrase to its normal meaning as synonymous with 'never'. That this is a trick need not be proved from general principles, since in the present context it is enough to point out that parallel reasoning from the same given (p always) would also yield the conclusion that for every (genuine) time t, it is impossible at t that p!)

In some such way, it might be thought, Aristotle starts from a collective 'always' in the given, and ends with an impossibility attaching distributively to each time taken singly. Had he started with the distributive sense and stuck to it throughout, the conclusion would never have seemed plausible. For if 'always' is taken distributively, "the" given, that X is always F, must be treated in effect as a series of givens each referring to a moment or finite period within "all time"; and at any of these times taken one by one it may be possible that X should be not-F at some other time, even though each is in fact a time when X is F. But if Aristotle failed to distinguish the senses of 'all' he could perhaps have got B' to his own satisfaction by the spurious reasoning reconstructed above.

That reconstruction is not entirely on the wrong track. It is true that Aristotle interprets 'X is always F' as referring to the totality of time: and from this he does deduce that at each moment it is impossible that X should ever not be F. But behind this, I shall argue, lies something rather more interesting than undisciplined confusion about different senses of 'all'.

At I.11, 281a8 ff., he laid it down that capacities in the primary sense should be defined with reference to the maximum exercise. He was not, as we have said, speaking of capacities in general, but of those for *being*, in the sense spelt out in the doctrine of the categories. But he does imply that *all* capacities for being (in this sense) are maximum-related. Now in 12 he draws the contrast between things that are and are not at different times, and things that either always are or always are not. In all these occurrences 'are'/'are not' must be understood as completed by an 'F' in one of the categories. Furthermore, he speaks of *capacities* for being/not being F in connection with both sorts of case, the omnitemporal and the intermittent. An object that is always F is exercising a capacity for F-ness, no less than one that is F for a limited time. It follows from these remarks that his rule about defining with reference to the maximum covers capacities exercised by objects that are always F or always not-F. The presumption must be that he thinks of these capacities too as maximum-related. And as with the intermittently F objects, the maximum would be temporal. Hence an object that is always F/not-F is exercising a capacity such that the exercise has an inherent temporal maximum. But if the maximum were less than all of time the object would not be always as it is. So the maximum must be: all time. 'All time', in other words, is here to mean an *amount* of time—the greatest amount.

In *De Caelo* I.12 he equates being always F with being F for an infinite time. (See, e.g., 281a33–282a4, where the proof of imperishability and ingenerability is mainly conducted with the phrase 'for an infinite time', while the conclusions are drawn at 281b25 and 282a3 in terms of 'always'.) And near the beginning he speaks of infinite time as though it were an amount of time. He says that it is not numerically specifiable ('. . . μὴ ποσός τις'), but is 'greater than any that could be stated and lesser than none' (281a33–4). Thus he denies that it is measurable, yet speaks of it as *greater* than measurable amounts. But this suggests that he thinks of infinite time too as *an amount* (an immeasurable one). For it makes no sense to say that such and such an amount is lesser than. . . unless the other term of the comparison is also regarded as an amount.

The clearest evidence is at 283a4 ff. He has just been arguing that whatever has a beginning has an end, and conversely. (Thus 'for a finite time' and 'always' cover all the possibilities). But might there not be something that begins to be F and continues so for ever, or ceases to be so, having always been: so that for it there would only be a single beginning or a single ceasing, by contrast with the recurrent starts and stops of finite states with finite contradictories? This objection, he says (lines 6-7), can be met from a premiss already laid down. For, he continues:

All things capable of acting or suffering, of being or not being, are capable of these for a determinate (ὡρίσμενον) time, either infinite or of a specifiable amount (ποσόν). This applies to infinite time because infinite time is in a way determinate (ὥρισται πῶς) in so far as it is that than which none is greater. But what is infinite in one direction only is neither infinite nor determinate. (283a 7-10)[19]

That is: the one-way infinite is not determinate in the standard sense which entails 'finite'. But nor is it infinite in the sense of being lesser than none; hence it is not even 'in a way determinate'. Thus it is not (given the premiss) a possible duration for a categorizable F-state. The premiss is repeated in the first line of the quoted passage: it was stated first at 12, 281a28-30, having been prepared for in Chapter 11.

The logical point here is that a term 'D' denotes a determinate duration if and only if no two states of affairs can be truly said each to last for D unless their durations are equal. If 'equal' is taken to mean not merely 'of the same number of units' but 'such that neither is longer than the other', then 'always' and 'for infinite time both ways' are like phrases such as 'for five hours': they stand for determinate durations. Whereas 'for time infinite one way' does not, since of two conditions without end or without beginning, one might have begun or might cease sooner than the other, in which case it would be 'in a way' longer or shorter.

---

[19] I take 'ὡρίσμενον' in line 7 as applying to 'ἄπειρον' as well as to 'ποσόν'. It is grammatically possible to take it with 'ποσόν' alone; which would give a completely uniform meaning with the occurrence in 10. But this makes the argument unintelligible. And in the earlier statement of the premiss (281a28-30) 'ὡρίσμενον' occurs without 'ποσόν'. Again, 9-10 are sometimes translated (e.g. by J.L. Stocks, Oxford) as: 'infinite time is in a fashion *defined* as that than which none is greater'. But this too is inconsequential, and in any case 'ὡρίσμενον' at 7 and 10 cannot mean 'defined'.

But Aristotle, I think, also has in mind here another and a more controversial sense of 'determinate duration', implying 'whole' or 'complete'. He is not speaking of time in the abstract, but of the time for being or not-being, doing or suffering, by some particular individual in a specific respect. Now, a finite length of time will of course be a *whole* day or minute, or a whole thirty-three hours, etc.; and in this sense all time and infinite time cannot be a whole. It is not, in other words, a whole so and so where 'so and so' specifies a unit or sum of units of measurement. However, the finite time of something's being F (where the duration is inherently limited) is the time which the object takes to exercise its F-capacity to the *full*. For the capacity is defined with reference to just this temporal limit. Hence although the maximum period will be so many days, etc. (say, a whole year), it is not *qua* having lasted this measure of time that X's F-ness ceases when it does, but *qua* having worked itself out to the full. For other objects of other kinds may be F for some longer period; hence it is not because in one case F-ness in the abstract has lasted for a year that in this case it gives way to its contradictory, but because *this* object's F-ness is geared to continue that long, thus fully realizing *its* particular capacity.[20] In this sense of 'whole' it is perhaps not so absurd to think of *all time* too as a sort of whole, i.e. as the time required for the full exercise of certain capacities by certain particular beings. The point is reinforced if we consider what is implied by the notion of inherent temporal restriction even in finite cases. If the duration really is *inherently* limited, its boundedness does not consist primarily in the fact that *some other state will follow*, but in the fact that this F-ness has (for this occasion) played itself out. Then of course some other state will replace it. But one might almost say that this is accidental. If, speaking absurdly, time were to end just then so that nothing else followed, it would still be true that the F-ness had brought itself to a close. Boundedness in this sense does not depend on something's coming *after*. Thus all time (the "life-span" of certain

---

[20] Cf. 11, 281a11–12 and 19: 'δέον ὁρίζεσθαι πρὸς τὸ τέλος καὶ τὴν ὑπεροχὴν τὴν δύναμιν'.

things) may also be regarded as a *period*, even though *ex vi termini* the condition is lacking for calling it 'limited' in the familiar sense.[21]

Since the specification of the maximum ought to appear in a full definition of a capacity (as possessed by a given subject), something that is always F is not simply always exercising the capacity for being F: it is exercising the capacity for being-F-always.[22] And at each moment of exercise it is exercising *that* capacity. (That is not to say that at each moment it is always F. A man who can lift up to two hundred pounds is exercising this capacity on every pound he lifts, but he does not on that account lift two hundred pounds for every pound he lifts.) And not only is the same capacity for being-F-always exercised at every moment of time, but one and the same *exercise* occupies this time. If a man lifts a weight of a hundred pounds, we do not say that he is exercising twice over, or displaying two exercises, of the capacity to lift fifty. This would imply that fifty is his maximum, which contradicts the supposition that he lifts a hundred. Similarly, although the always-F object is F from t_m to t_n, from t_n to t_o, t_o to t_p, etc., it does not engage in different exercises for each of these periods. To say this would imply that each period held a complete exercise which was then immediately repeated. But this contradicts the

[21] It may be wondered why, if there is no conceptual conflict for Aristotle between infinity and determinacy, he does not hold the universe to be infinite in size as well as duration. It is a sphere of concentric shells of which one is *the largest*, and there is neither space nor matter beyond it. (It is as if the sphere has only an inner surface). Thus it is of definite shape, and there is 'nothing greater'. Why then not infinite, unless because infinity and determinacy are incompatible? In fact all Aristotle's arguments for spatial finitude start from the premiss that the outermost shell (of the fixed stars) revolves at a constant rate, completing the revolution in a finite time. If the universe were infinite yet still a sphere, the outermost shell would describe a circle of infinite circumference, and each point on the physical periphery would traverse this length within a finite time, since revolutions are completed. But: 'nothing can traverse an infinite distance in a finite time'. (*De Caelo* I.5) Two points in this bear out our account of infinite *time* as a determinate whole. First, in the spatial case too there is no conflict between determinacy (of shape) and 'having nothing beyond it'. Secondly, Aristotle's reason for denying spatial infinity rests on the *motion* of the whole, which in the case of a temporal whole does not arise.

[22] On the textual plausibility of this interpretation see Williams, pp. 103 ff. He points out that Aquinas in his commentary takes 'always' as qualifying 'being' (i.e. 'being F'): in other words, as qualifying what the capacity is a capacity *for*.

hypothesis that the inherent maximum is all time. Thus under the present interpretation we cannot view the always-F as successively performing distinct finite acts of being F. It is now not at all obvious that it can still be viewed in the way that allows purchase for that distributive sense of 'all time' which earlier seemed to spell the downfall of Aristotle's argument. If there were a series of finitely enduring F-states, then given each, the non-occurrence of the next is not absurd. As it is, the always-F-ness, if given at all, is given as always-F-ness; and there cannot be more than one given, since there is not the time available for more than one exercise of the capacity. Although on the present interpretation we reject the distributive sense of 'all', it would not be strictly true to say that we accept the collective instead. 'Collection' suggests a plurality. But being always-F is a single exercise of a single capacity, and as such marks off the time it takes as a single time. There begins to be a certain plausibility in Aristotle's assumption that there is no time to which the supposition 'X is not F' can be coherently referred so as to exhibit it as ever possible.

However, the man who can lift up to two hundred pounds may exercise his power without exercising it in full. Should we not say that the same must be possible for the capacity of always-F-ness? Through interference a finitely timed process may not run its course, yet for reasons mentioned earlier even a partial realization must be described with reference to the full time. Should we not say then that an object that is now and always has been exercising the capacity for being always-F might nevertheless cease to exercise it, since interference has not been logically ruled out? And since being always-F is this object's way of being F (because *ex hypothesi* it is not finitely-F[23]), in ceasing from this it would cease to be F altogether. This, it would seem, is the weak point of the argument. But Aristotle is able to cover it if he is permitted the assumption that every categorizable state, negative as well as positive, is of an inherently determinate duration, whether finite or infinite. He must also assume that for any given object capacities are constant. But

---

[23] I.e. exercising the capacity for being F-finitely.

on this basis it can be shown that whatever is (ever) always-F (or always-not-F) cannot cease to be F (or not -F.

We begin from the consideration that a so-called possibility (or, in the abstract sense, capacity) cannot be regarded as existing or obtaining as a genuine possibility when the conditions logically exclude realization. For example: something which is not-F (or F) has no possibility of *beginning* to be always-F (or always-not-F), for on those terms there is, for that object, no such possibility. This is because if X was ever not-F it cannot ever subsequently exercise to the full a capacity for being always-F, since a full exercise requires all time, which by construction is not now available. For if the conditions are such that a capacity that is defined by reference to a certain maximal exercise *cannot* be maximally exercised, then at most there exists only a capacity for some lesser maximum. It follows that the only states that can begin are those constituted by exercises of capacities for finite exercise. What can begin must be of a nature to cease; hence what can begin once must also recur (since its contradictory, too, can—and must—begin, and so is of a nature to cease).

The impossibility that an always-state (negative or positive) should have begun entails that it cannot cease either, even through interference, provided it is assumed that capacities are constant. Suppose that an exercise of always-F-ness is interrupted so that X becomes not-F. Then it must begin to be either finitely- or always-not-F. But the latter is impossible. But so is the former, since finite-not-F-ness must give way to finite-F-ness. That would be possible only if X had always had the capacity for being finitely-F; but in that case its F-maximum was never 'always' (since one maximum excludes another), and X was never exercising always-F-ness: which denies the hypothesis.

So, if it is ever the case that X is always-F then X must always remain and must always have been always-F. And since what is always-F is *a fortiori* F, X must always be and have been F. The last clause means: 'It never has been nor will be the case that X has an unrealized possibility for being not-F'. For (1) if X is ever F in any way at all, it follows that it never had or will have the unrealized possibility of being always-not-F, since this type of possibility is totally absent except where completely realized. And (2) if X is ever always-F, then it never had or will have the possibility of being finitely-not-F, since although in general this can belong without at the time being realized, it is yoked with the positive finite capacity, and the latter has no purchase in a subject endowed with the positive *always*-capacity.[24]

At last, then, we can derive proposition B′: 'If it is always the case that *p*, then necessarily *p*'. Like A′ above, this holds only where '*p*' is a predication in a category. So: (since '*p*' = 'X is F/not-F' for categorizable 'F') (1) 'It is always the case that *p*' entails, on *De Caelo* principles, (2) 'X is always-F/-not-F'; and this in turn entails (3) 'It never has been and never will be possible that X is ever not-F/F', i.e. (4) 'It is always necessary that always *p*'. Thus if it is always the case that *p*, then '*p*' is in the strongest sense necessary. And this necessity, it is now clear, is strongest not in any undefined sense, but in that formulated earlier in terms of the *De Caelo* logical rule for relative temporalized possibility.[25] B′, then, is an RT-result reached by means of that rule. But not by the rule alone: for other principles were needed too. These we have located in the text, and have shown them to be metaphysical rather than logical in nature.[26]

We are left with a puzzling fact. It seems that B′, or some version of it, is a constant element in Aristotle's philosophy,

---

[24] But might not X cease to exercise always-F-ness if through interference it simply ceased to exist? Our argument relies only on the impossibility of its acquiring either form of not-F-ness. But for Aristotle unpropertied non-existence is not a possibility. Whatever ceases to be turns into something else.

[25] See above, Ch. III.

[26] *De Caelo* I.10, 280a32–4 and 12, 283b17 are sometimes taken to mean that Aristotle regards the proof of B′ as purely logical, i.e. as not resting on metaphysical considerations. See, e.g., Williams, pp. 212 ff. But what Aristotle actually says is (a) that it is universal, i.e. does not apply only to the heavens, and (b) that it does not rely on considerations drawn from natural science ('φυσικῶς'). Were he to depend on these there would be no need to deal with the question of interference as possibly ending an exercise of always-F-ness. For to him the only objects with omnitemporal properties are in fact the celestial spheres, and for cosmological reasons these are beyond reach of interference. In I.11–12 he ignores such physical facts, but this is not to say that the argument there proceeds on logical (formal) principles alone: nor does he say that it does. The distinction I make here between logic and metaphysics is important for answering the question raised in the Introduction: Are A′ and B′ analytic or synthetic? (See pp. 4 ff.)

as is the organic notion of substance on which it is based. We might suppose him to have had second thoughts about the spurious parallelism of assigning to negative conditions temporal maxima in common with their positive counterparts, although I know of no evidence for this. But there is another assumption which he definitely rejects at some stage. This is that 'infinite time' means 'the whole of time'. In *Physics* III.6 he writes:

It turns out that the infinite is the opposite of what people say. For it is not that which has nothing beyond it. No, the infinite is that which has always something of itself beyond it . . . . The infinite, then, is that of which, in taking a specific amount (κατὰ ποσὸν λαμβάνουσιν) we always leave something more to take. Whereas that of which there is nothing beyond is complete and whole. For we define a whole as that from which there is nothing absent, like a whole man or box. What is true in each particular application is true of wholes as such: the whole is that no part of which lies outside it. That which has some part missing outside it is not an 'all' (πᾶν), whatever the absent element may be [i.e. however small]. The 'whole' and the 'complete' are either just the same or very similar in nature. But nothing is complete that has no end, and the end is a limit . . . . [The infinite] *qua* infinite does not contain but is contained [i.e. exceeded]. (206b33-207a25.)

Does Aristotle count his earlier self among 'the people' mentioned in the first sentence? He does not say; and it is not even certain that this passage was written after *De Caelo* I.12.[27] Let us leave aside the question whether *Physics* III represents a conscious advance on the view of *De Caelo* I.12, or alternatively on a view to which a later *De Caelo* I.12 quietly reverts. Let us simply consider how the *Physics* analysis affects his argument for B'. Once it is admitted that 'infinite time' means 'a time for which there is always a further time', i.e. 'a series of finite times each bounded by

---

[27] It is tempting to see the more sophisticated account of infinity in the *Physics* as postdating *De Caelo* I.12. However, Aristotle frequently refers in *De Caelo* to passages in *Physics* III as if to an earlier work (see Guthrie's Introduction to the Loeb edition, pp. xxviii-xxix). The most striking reference for the present discussion is at II.4, 286b18-20, where he alludes to the analysis of 'complete' given in the *Physics* passage just quoted. Such references may, however, be later additions to a pre-*Physics* III original. But if he went over *De Caelo* in the light of a later *Physics* III, how could he miss the discrepancy between the later and earlier treatments of 'infinite'? There is as much of a puzzle here as if we suppose *Physics* III to be the earlier work.

another', then if 'always' is taken as equivalent to 'for infinite
time', the sentence 'X is always F' means only 'For each of
an infinite series of finite times, X exercises the capacity for
being F'. The capacity itself cannot now be defined by
reference to infinite time, since this made sense only in so far
as the latter was treated as a maximal amount logically
parallel with finite spans. But it was only by attaching infinity to the capacity, and to the F-ness for which this is a
capacity, that we were able to treat 'X is F for infinite time'
as expressing a single given fact. On the *Physics* III.6 interpretation, 'X is F for infinite time' presents a series of givens
distinguished by whatever finite unit of time we care to
apply; and in relation to each of these the subsequent ceasing
to be F can now be proved possible.

But Aristotle was not necessarily inconsistent in maintaining B′ (as a rational position) even at a time when he
denied one of the assumptions essential to the *De Caelo*
proof. The *Physics* analysis of 'infinite' tells against that
proof only if 'always' and 'for an infinite time' are made
synonymous. He could have dropped the synonymy and
kept 'always' as meaning 'for the whole of time': in that
case the *De Caelo* argument goes through, if 'always' is read
throughout. In the *Physics* passage quoted, the sentence
'That which has some part missing outside it is not an "all"'
suggests a move in this direction.[28] But reconciliation on
these lines generates a new problem. The infinity of time, in
whatever sense of 'infinite', is another of Aristotle's constant doctrines. Hence whatever lasts always is taken to last
for infinite time, even if 'always' and 'for infinite time' do
not mean the same. But if 'always' implies a whole, while
'infinite' excludes this, and if the same duration is to be
described by both terms, it follows that this duration is to
be regarded both as a whole and as an uncompletable series
of finite stretches.

---

[28] If the direction is followed, we should expect to find statements of the *De
Caelo* position in which 'ἀεί' and 'ἀίδιον' occur, but not 'τὸν ἄπειρον χρόνον'. In
fact this seems to be the rule. See e.g. *De Int.* 9, 19a9 and 35–6; *Phys.* III.4,
203b30 (where the reference to infinite body is beside the point); *De Gen. et
Corr.* II.9, 335a33–4 and 11, 338a1–3; *Metaph.* E.2, 1026b27–8; Θ.8, 1050b7 ff.
(cf. ibid. 6, 1048b9 ff. for a statement of *Phys.* III.6 conclusions); K.8, 1064b
32–3; N.2, 1088b23–5.

Perhaps the answer to that paradox lies in a distinction between time in the abstract and the time of an activity or state. I shall not pursue the question here; Aristotle gives no clear lead. For the sake of B′ he does not need to. There are Aristotelian grounds for B′ which so far have not been mentioned; and they do not directly involve the concept of temporal maxima. Hence 'for an infinite time' may stand in for 'always' even if taken in the sense of *Physics* III. I shall come to this in the seventh chapter. Meanwhile we have not yet finished with Aristotle's formal concept of possibility. Its contribution to *De Caelo* I.12 has now been made clear. It remains to view its performance in another battlefield: that of *De Interpretatione* 9.

V

De Interpretatione 9

In *De Interpretatione* 9 Aristotle argues that if a certain
logical principle is maintained without restriction, we face
the consequence that nothing is contingent: all events happen
with a necessity that makes planning and deliberation pointless and leaves no rational basis for our sense of our own
agency. For we see ourselves as agents so far as we see ourselves as bringing about one of a set of alternatives each of
which is possible, so that what we do make happen is not the
only thing that could have happened. The connection between
agency and a range of possible alternatives is perhaps most
clearly to the fore in cases where a person deliberates,[1] since
no doubt it is when faced with a problem of decision that we
are most sharply aware of the different possibilities available:
that they are different and that they are all possibilities. But
even when there is no deliberation, whether through lack of
time or because it is unnecessary or through carelessness, the
connection still holds, just to the extent to which the agent
sees himself as realizing a state of affairs that might not have
been realized. Such a view of ourselves, in Aristotle's opinion,
we should be forced to discard as false and deluded unless we
are prepared to limit the scope of the logical principle first
mentioned. He argues, therefore, that it must be restricted so
as not to apply to certain future-tensed statements about particulars: those, namely, that represent contingencies whose
realization one way or the other lies within the power of the
human agent.

In broad terms this is the reasoning of *De Interpretatione*
9. But every detail within this outline remains the subject of
unsparing debate after two thousand years. What is the logical
principle which must be restricted? Why, if not, does it
threaten contingency? What concept of contingency is at

---

[1] Cf. *De Int.* 9, 18b31; 19a9.

issue here? Is Aristotle confused? Or, if we cannot readily translate his reasoning into any line of thought that we our- selves find compelling, is this because he operates with strange rules and concepts? It is not to be expected that these questions will be answered to the satisfaction of all; but they cannot be set aside by anyone claiming to have ex- tracted a coherent set of modal concepts from *De Caelo* I.12. It may be wondered, for instance, why *De Interpretatione* 9 is so difficult to follow, if Aristotle's formal modal thinking elsewhere is as clear as I have argued it to be. Is it that in the present passage he uses modalities of a different sort, or is he handling the same ones in ways of which my earlier analysis takes no account? And if, either way, there operates here some modally relevant factor not yet identified, then perhaps this was present also in *De Caelo* I.12, making an un- detected contribution to the proof of A′ and B′. In particular I have in mind the question whether the view of contingency worked out by Aristotle in *De Interpretatione* 9 entails the concept of a third truth-value. Many scholars have followed Łukasiewicz in thinking so.[2] If they are right, then to the extent to which the modalities there coincide with those of *De Caelo* I.12, my discussion of the latter overlooks an important element whose failure to surface in the text itself cannot now be taken at face value.

In *De Interpretatione* 9 the interpreter's problem is to identify Aristotle's problem. As long as this seems to centre on *modality* our previous results remain doubtful. However I shall argue in this chapter that Aristotle's trouble has a different source. All the evidence suggests that his modal concepts here are identical with the RT-concepts studied earlier. But on the view to be proposed below, it is not necessary to suppose these any less straightforward than they earlier seemed, in order to explain *De Interpretatione* 9.

I must stress that by 'RT-concepts' I mean those which emerged in Chapters II and III through analysis of Aristotle's formal rule for determining possibility in *De Caelo* I.12. These notions must be distinguished from the metaphysically interpreted subject-matter on which in that context Aristotle

---

[2] Recently, e.g., Jeffrey, op. cit.

brings them to bear. The distinction is clear, because the metaphysical interpretation applies only to predications in the categories, while the formal rule for 'possible' has a wider range. But if the narrow scope of the propositions A′ and B′ is overlooked, it will seem that in *De Interpretatione* 9 Aristotle undertakes a task logically impossible for him to fulfil as long as he clings to the results of *De Caelo* I.12. That task is to uphold the common-sense presumption that some situations are within human power to produce or prevent as willed. But on the metaphysical basis for A′ and B′ in *De Caelo* I.12, despite its contrast between the necessary and the contingent, there is no room for such situations. The contingencies falling under A′ are not up to human agents to bring about or avoid. They are called 'contingent' because their future occurrence and their future non-occurrence are each consistent with the actual state of things at any given time. But it is also metaphysically inevitable that both possibilities be for ever alternately realized at more or less fixed intervals. The sort of biological and meteorological sequences that fill this bill are as independent of human intervention as the continuous and necessary heavenly motions from which their regularity derives.[3] If it is believed that Aristotle intends A′ to cover all the cases, or even all the types of case, to which it makes sense to apply the formal rule for 'possible', the only possible conclusion will be that he lacks an integrated modal theory. For on this view the two passages directly contradict each other if the basic meaning of 'contingent' is the same in both;[4] and if it is not, we are left with two sets of modal concepts whose difference and mutual relations Aristotle never explains.

But in fact many possibilities lie outside the scope of A′: not merely for change and modes of ceasing, as we saw,[5] but also for a large class of relatively stable conditions. These are conditions involving the combined operations of distinct substances, or, if we prefer, conditions considered from a point

---

[3] *De Gen. et Corr.*, II.10–11.

[4] They might be reconcilable on the assumption that the occurrence and non-occurrence of volitions is predetermined like everything else. But Aristotle sees the will as an initiating cause.

[5] See pp. 61 ff.

of view from which reference to more than one substance is, for whatever reason, relevant. While it may be inherent in X to be and to continue to be F for just so long, it does not follow that the *circumstances* of the F-ness on any given occasion are regulated from within like its duration. The circumstances depend on other substances following also their own natures, but how these unfoldings on various occasions are conjoined in space and time is not up to the individual nature of any: nor for Aristotle is there any super-substance that co-ordinates in every detail the behaviour of the others. His highest substances, the heavens and the un-moved mover, provide by their operation the *general* con-ditions (physical and metaphysical) for the regular function-ing of the rest; but that is all. No doubt various states of a single organism are geared from within to coincide, so that their coincidence will fall under A'. But the universe as whole is not a single organism.

Thus coincidences take place which are accidental to the natures of the objects involved, and here if anywhere there is scope for chance and also for human agency: whether in putting things together and taking them apart, as in the construction of artefacts, or in timing events to avoid or overlap with others, as in practical activity in general. In deliberating whether to fight a sea-battle tomorrow, what is at issue is not whether we should fight or not *simpliciter*, nor on a certain date abstractly conceived, but whether to fight under the conditions which, given the present state of things, may be expected to obtain a few hours from now. These conditions are relevant not merely negatively, as per-mitting the event (which would be their only point of in-terest if we were describing or explaining the natural beha-viour of some single substance), but as giving it its particular significance as a possible object of choice for this agent on this occasion. For although 'tomorrow' comes into the picture because of the circumstances forecast for then, this indexical reference to a particular time cannot be replaced by a description of the circumstances in purely general terms so that the question would become: 'Shall we fight a sea-battle under such and such conditions?' The agent as such is concerned not simply that so and so be realized at some time or other, but with its realization by steps beginning now. Hence he sees what he aims for as occurring (if achieved) at or by some assignable time from now. The assignment may not be precise (e.g. if he does not know how long is needed) but it cannot, logically, be left on entirely open question. Thus it is that in *De Interpretatione* 9 Aristotle uses the sentences 'There will be/will not be a sea-battle *tomorrow*' to illustrate the sort of contingency he believes to be jeopardized by a certain logical rule. As a practical option the battle must be contingent in all its particularity, not merely as involving particular individuals, but as occurring at or by some particular time marked out by reference to its distance from the present.

There can be little doubt that Aristotle here gives to 'contingent' essentially the same logical meaning as it bears in *De Caelo* I.12, the difference being that there the sentences were not dated.[6] Thus to say that a battle on a particular day is contingent is to say that at some earlier time the state of things was such that it was possible then that there would be, and also that there would not be, a battle on the day in question. The supposition used in applying the RT rule would be either that the undated 'There is a battle' will be true on the day mentioned, or that the dated 'There is a battle on day D' is (simply) true. The evidence for construing 'contingent' in *De Interpretatione* 9 as 'RT-contingent' lies partly in the detail of the text and partly in wider considerations. Thus, for instance, in the chapter itself he formulates his thesis in alternative ways that are equivalent in RT-terms but not obviously so on any other hypothesis. He begins by stating that the troublesome logical principle does not in general cover *future-tensed* statements about particulars, although past- and present-tensed ones fall under it (18a33 ff.), and ends by stating that it does not cover what is *contingent* (19a36–b4). The implication is that contingent statements essentially refer to the future. In RT-terms this makes perfect sense when the sentences are dated. 'p/t' is either necessary or impossible at t itself, and for all times subsequent to t the question whether 'p/t' is now contingent

---

[6] 'For a finite time' etc. gives a length of time, not a date.

cannot arise. Hence '*p/t*' is contingent (if at all) only for as long as it refers to a future time. Again, throughout he writes as if his defence of *contingency* is a sufficient defence of human agency. From the standpoint of someone who views all modality as relative to actual situations this is logical enough, for as ordinarily understood, the statement 'I could have brought about something different' means: 'The actual situation from which I started to act was such that different options were *then* open'. But if the occurrence were to be called 'contingent' on the ground simply that the negation of the sentence reporting it is logically self-consistent, or that we can conceive of a world sharing no part of its history with ours in which no such thing takes place, then an argument proving that some things are genuinely contingent in either of these ways might perhaps serve to show that a creative deity could have done otherwise, but not that any human agent could, in the sense of 'could' built into our ordinary notion of agency.

Since Aristotle equates contingency as such with RT-contingency, the determinism he opposes in *De Interpretatione* 9 is the most stringent possible. In his eyes it means that there is *no* sense in which anything could happen that does not happen. He cannot, logically, entertain the idea that there might have been a world with different physical laws from those actually prevailing. Nor is it open to him to say that for any given event the boundary conditions might have been different, so that a different inevitable outcome might have ensued. For if things have always been such that it was never possible that tomorrow's battle would not take place, then boundary conditions permitting its non-occurrence have never existed in the history of this world: and in RT-terms no other is conceivably possible. The Aristotelian determinist would admit, of course, that under different conditions it would have been possible or even necessary that the battle would not take place. But this does not imply that the actual battle *is* in any sense contingent. Its non-occurrence *is* in no way possible unless it *has* been possible for the boundary conditions to be other than they are, which is ruled out *ex hypothesi*. To say that so and so would be or have been possible *if . . .* is not to say that it *is* or ever *was* possible—

unless we wish to argue that it *is* possible that the diagonal of the square be commensurate with the side, on the ground that it *would* be possible *if* natural numbers were both odd and even.[7] Thus the determinism envisaged by Aristotle would give every empirical truth the same necessity as a mathematical conclusion from first principles.

De Interpretatione 9 falls into three parts. Aristotle first argues that a certain logical rule (let us label it 'L') applies to singular statements about the past and present, but cannot apply to all concerning the future, since that would wipe out contingency (18a28-b25). Next he underlines the consequences of its universal application, and their absurdity: deliberation would be pointless, and events would have been necessary in advance for ten thousand years and more; all of which is unacceptable, since deliberation and agency do initiate events, and not everything that happens has to. E.g. I shall in fact keep my coat until it wears out, but this is not its only possible fate; it might be cut up first although it will not be (18b26-19a22). Thirdly, he shows that it is only through a fallacious use of the term 'necessary' that we seem to have any reason to think everything necessary. This final section ends with the affirmation that contingent statements lie outside the scope of L (19a23-b4).

The main problem for exegesis lies in the first section and its relation to the third. On the most natural interpretation L is not a principle that raises any obvious problem for contingency; nor is it clear how its universal application generates, depends on, or is otherwise relevant to the fallacies dissolved towards the end of the chapter.

In Aristotle's own opening words, L is as follows: 'It is necessary that either the affirmation or the denial be true or false' (18a28-9). Since L is some kind of logical principle, 'necessary' here in RT-terms must mean: 'There has never been a time when it was possible that the negation should ever be true'. Now from the initial formulation L could be taken as enjoining the ascription of one or other truth-value to at least one side of any affirmation/denial pair of statements. In that case the rule would be satisfied even if one

[7] Cf. *An. Pr.* I.23, 41a26f.

side were assigned no value, or a third "neuter" one. However it rapidly becomes clear that this is not what Aristotle means by L, but rather that for every pair, one side must (in the strongest sense) be true and the other false. This is shown in his sentence summing up the first section (18b 26–31), and it is this rule whose universal application he takes himself to have refuted by the end of the chapter, where he says: 'So it is clear that it is not necessary that in every affirmation/denial antithesis one side be true *and* the other false' (19a39–b2; my emphasis).

What are we to make of the position of 'necessary' in L? On the natural reading of both formulations just quoted, we have a necessary complex proposition, not a complex of necessary propositions. Later in the chapter (19a28ff.) Aristotle shows himself very much alive to the possibility of confusing two such forms. He asserts that the Law of Excluded Middle holds even for contingent future events, i.e. that it is necessary, for instance, that there will be or will not be a sea-battle tomorrow, but: 'we must not divide and say that either one is necessary'. Here he speaks in the material mode: neither *event* is necessary, although their disjunction is. But he immediately goes on to say that the same applies to propositions or statements: the statements corresponding to the events are contingent as statements, i.e. neither is necessarily true, even though the disjunction itself is a necessary truth.

Aristotle's evident awareness that the necessity of a complex (whether this be a fact or a proposition) cannot automatically be distributed over the elements, is the source of much of the puzzlement hanging over this chapter. For in the first place his clarity on this point would appear to authorize a straightforward interpretation of L according to which the 'necessary' in that formula has just the scope it seems to have, viz. the whole clause: 'one side of the antithesis is true, the other false'. Surely if he had meant L as a principle according to which one side is necessarily true and the other necessarily false, he not only could but would have made his meaning clear, not smothering it up in a form of words which he well knows says something different. Secondly, not only can we not take L to *mean* 'One side is necessarily true, the other necessarily false', but the same considerations make it equally implausible that he sees it as *entailing* this proposition. But in that case, why does he think that L must be restricted in order to allow for contingency? If we forget about his remarks at 19a28ff., the argument in the first section reads like a perfect example of the fallacy of division committed with 'necessarily' (in the strongest sense):

If every affirmation or denial is true or false, everything necessarily is or is not the case. For suppose one man says that something will be, and another denies this very thing: it is clear that one of them is saying something true, if every affirmation is true or false. For on this assumption both things will not be the case at once. For if it is true to say that something is white or not white, it must be white or not white, and if it is white or not white, then it was true to affirm or deny this. And if it is not the case, the man's statement is false, and if it is false, what he says is not the case. So it is necessary that the affirmation or the denial be true. So nothing either is or comes about or will be or not be by chance or whichever way it chanced, but everything is of necessity and not whichever way it chanced, since either the man who affirms or the one who denies is speaking the truth. (18a34–b8.)

Up to the last sentence every remark can be understood as correctly inferred from 'Necessarily one is true and the other false'. Then suddenly we get what to us seems a new and un-grounded direction, and the obvious explanation for this is not available, by Aristotle's own showing later in the chapter. It may be thought that in this first section he is not speaking for himself but presenting the case of a confused thinker who has either unknowingly shifted the necessity operator or believes the shift to be legitimate. But if this is what Aristotle is up to, then when he later explodes the fallacy of division his next move would surely be to point out that L, even when unrestricted, poses no problem for contingency. Yet this is exactly what he does not do: for at the very end of the discussion, when all the relevant fallacies have in his view been unravelled, he declares again that contingencies do not fall within the scope of L, on the ground that if they did they would not be contingencies.

Leaving aside for the moment the problem of explaining this sequence of thought, let us consider more closely what logical principle it is that L on the natural interpretation is intended to convey. It is not the Law of Excluded Middle

(LEM), 'Necessarily, either p or not-p', since this does not feature the semantic concepts 'true' and 'false'; and in any case we have seen how in 19a28 ff. Aristotle is clear that he does not propose to restrict the LEM, and that his argument does not require it. But nor is L exactly the Law of Bivalence (LB), 'Necessarily, every statement is either true or false', for this is expressed without reference to antithetical pairs. However, L follows from conjoining LB with the assumption that the two sides of an antithesis are not both true or both false.

Thus anyone who denies or restricts L may be doing so on any one of several grounds. He may hold (a) that some statements are neither true nor false, and this may be (a') because he holds that for some antitheses, neither side has either truth-value, or (a'') because he holds that for some, one side lacks both. Or he may hold (b) that in some antitheses the two sides may be (b') both true or (b'') both false. Those commentators who accept the natural interpretation of L have generally supposed Aristotle to be rejecting L for reason (a'). For it seems incredible that he should have maintained (b') or (b'') for any antithetical pairs, and in any case in 18b15–25 he explicitly argues against (b''). As for (a''), it appears to be taken for granted that the two sides of an antithesis are symmetrical as regards being or not being true-or-false.

However, a problem arises over (a'). How can Aristotle maintain LEM without restriction while holding that some future-tensed singulars lack truth-value? If either we shall or we shall not fight a sea-battle between noon and sunset tomorrow, how can it be that neither of the corresponding statements is true? Even though we do not know which, how can that affect the point that one or the other is, or will turn out to have been true, given that the event will either happen or not? Again, if it will either happen or not, it must be true that it will happen or not; and how can this disjunction be true unless one or other disjunct is?

Partly because of this difficulty, some commentators hold that despite appearances to the contrary, the L which Aristotle seems to restrict is: 'For all pairs, one side is (in the strongest sense) necessarily true and the other necessarily false'. On this interpretation, he does not deny truth and falsity to any future-tensed cases, but only (in some cases) necessary truth and necessary falsity. We will call this the 'SD' version of L, since it results from understanding L's apparently single occurrence of 'Necessary' *in sensu diviso*.

However, Aristotle evidently believes the unrestricted L, whatever he means by it, to be plausible enough for him to need to mount an argument against it. But the SD version makes a claim so audacious that the burden of proof, it would seem, lies with whoever proposes, not whoever rejects it. All the same, there are two fallacies by which it may seem to follow from unexceptionable premisses. These Aristotle considers in the third section. The first has already been mentioned: it is the erroneous division of 'Necessarily' prefacing the unrestricted LEM. I assume that Aristotle is thinking in terms of RT-necessity when he discusses this; but the error can just as well be committed and exposed in terms of non-temporalized necessity. This is not, I think, true of the other. Aristotle's words can be taken in more than one way, but on what I believe to be the correct interpretation they refer to a fallacy peculiar to users of RT-concepts. He writes:

That something that is should be whenever it is, and that something that is not should not be whenever it is not, is necessary. But not everything that is or is not, is or is not of necessity. For [to say] that everything necessarily is when it is, is not the same as [to say] that it necessarily is *simpliciter* (ἁπλῶς). Similarly for that which is not. (19a23-7.)

In one interpretation 'necessarily' has its strongest sense throughout, and the first sentence says (1): 'For all p, necessarily (p whenever p)'. Aristotle's point then is that this does not entail (2): 'For all p, if p then necessarily p', although it might seem so. On this reading '*simpliciter*' qualifies the single 'p' in the consequent of (2) and contrasts this with 'p when p' in (1). Alternatively, and I think preferably, we can take the first sentence as saying: (1'): 'For all p, whenever p, it is necessary then that p then', or in other words: 'For all p and all t, if p/t then it is necessary at t that p/t', which is a tautology in RT-terms.[8] In that case

---

[8] Cf. McCall, op. cit., pp. 429-30, and see above, pp. 39 ff.

Aristotle is saying that this does not (although it may seem
to) entail (2′): 'For all *p*, if *p/t* then it is always necessary
that *p/t*'. Here *'simpliciter'* qualifies 'necessarily' and means
'without restriction to any special time', and the contrast is
with 'necessary-at-*t*'.[9]

Aristotle first discusses both fallacies in first-order terms
of necessary being and non-being, and then in each case
stresses that exactly the same points hold good if necessity
is attributed to the corresponding statements (19a27-8 and
33-5). On this level the fallacies lead to the conclusion that
every statement is (in the strongest sense) necessarily true or
necessarily false, i.e. L on the SD interpretation. But Aristotle
counters:

Since the truth of statements matches the realities, it is clear that
whenever things are such as to be whichever way it chances, and contraries are each possible, the same must be true for the antithetical
statements. This is the case with things that are not everlasting, or
whose non-being is not everlasting. With them it is necessary that one
side of the antithetical pair be true or false, but not that it be this particular side or that; only that it be one or the other, whichever way it
chances . . . (19a33-8.)

The last sentence tails off into an obscurity which we shall
discuss later. But even so these remarks[10] pose a severe difficulty for anyone who thinks that the message of *De Interpretatione* 9 is that truth and falsity ought to be denied to
future-tensed contingents. For here he is surely saying that
it is necessary that one side or other be true, and the other
false, but contingent which is which.

Thus first and last, it seems, the SD interpretation of L
makes best sense of the chapter. Such a position in its unrestricted form could well have seemed plausible to a slip-
shod reasoner, especially one who shared but had not mastered
Aristotle's own notion of modality as temporalized and

---

[9] Since writing the above I find this interpretation supported by G.H. von
Wright in 'Time, Truth and Necessity', *Intention and Intentionality*, pp. 237-50.
On several points this paper confirms my view of Aristotelian modality, although
I differ on the diagnosis of the problem of future contingents. For yet another
interpretation of 19a23-7, that of Hintikka, see below, p. 122.

[10] Especially the first clause ('ἐπεὶ ὁμοίως οἱ λόγοι ἀληθεῖς ὥσπερ τὰ
πράγματα'), which can only mean that λόγοι are necessarily *or contingently* true
according as the facts are necessary or contingent.

relative to the actual. And in this form it genuinely eliminates contingency. Aristotle's proposed restriction does not clash with his maintaining the LEM universally; and it is consistent too with the remarks just quoted, where he seems to say that future contingents are (contingently) true or false.

Yet whenever Aristotle states L, at the beginning and the end and several times in between, he says: 'It is necessary that one side of the antithesis be true and the other false'. 'Necessary' is not openly distributed. For some, myself included, the powerful reasons in favour of treating it as if it were fail to tip the balance against the obstinate fact that it is not. In desperation we may start wondering whether Aristotle might have chosen his words with intent to baffle, perhaps to set readers the exercise of puzzling out for themselves what meanings would fit the argument. But such teasing maieusis is entirely out of keeping with the rest of *De Interpretatione* and uncharacteristic of Aristotle in general. And even Socrates can be relied on to show his hand in the end; but apparently not Aristotle here—unless he takes it to be plain enough all along, only for some reason the communication fails to reach us.

It is strange too, if L is meant *in sensu diviso*, that Aristotle should find it necessary to *argue*, and somewhat laboriously, that its unrestricted application does away with contingency. The reasoning for this occupies thirty-one lines, from 18a34 to b25: a long haul for demonstrating that 'Nothing is contingent' follows from 'Every statement is necessarily true or necessarily false'. Is this a very slow proof of a truism or rather too quick a one of something else?

Let us assume that 'Necessarily' in L is as undivided as the actual formulations suggest. Those who read it in this way generally think that Aristotle's restriction consists in the denial outright of prior truth-value to future-tensed contingents. But why should prior truth-value seem to eliminate contingency? One line of explanation might start from the fact that in determining contingency by the suppositional method, Aristotle has to assume that the present truth about what will happen is not part of the present situation-relative-to-which; for otherwise 'There will be a sea-battle tomorrow'

turns out as either necessary or impossible today.[11] The
assumption is not, as I have heard suggested, an *ad hoc* one
adduced to save the method from wholesale self-defeat: it
is not adduced at all, but already presupposed. For the
method is designed to test the possibility of what is not, or
not known to be, actual:[12] confronted by the known fact
that *p* we have no need to discover whether it is possible.
The method is as useless for this as a cure for a healthy man.
Thus however much we know about the situation-relative-to-
which some alleged contingency is up for testing, our premisses will not include the present truth of the relevant
future-tensed supposition—not because the method on this
inclusion would not work, but because we should have no
call to be working it. Nor could we ever get started if, not
knowing which of two future-tensed contradictories will
turn out to have been true, we nevertheless consider ourselves obliged to take into present account the truth of
whichever in fact *is* true. Thus the supposition under scrutiny
is *as if* neither true nor false for whoever conducts the
scrutiny. It may be that Aristotle finds it natural to couch
this epistemic point in realist terms, thus seeming to suspend a logical principle where all he needs is the fiction (in
certain contexts) of suspense.

If his reasoning is of this sort, essentially epistemic, there
is no inconsistency in his retaining the Law of Excluded
Middle unrestricted while (fictionally) denying truth or
falsity to future-tensed singulars. In wondering what futures
are possible as of now, we keep within the bounds set by
logic, so that, for instance, the question of a third option
between two contradictories is not up for consideration. It
is as if (for the reasons given) it is neither true nor false that
we shall fight tomorrow, and it is as if it is neither true nor
false that we shall not; but it is not as if we shall neither fight
nor not, nor as if the disjunction is not true: on the contrary,
both in determining what the possibilities are and in deciding
which to follow we take its truth for granted. And if a logician presses us to admit that in that case we effectively take
it for granted that one-or-other disjunct is now true and one

---

[11] Cf. pp. 50 ff.   [12] See pp. 16 ff.

false, we need not demur; for the point is only that we operate as if this were not the case.

The explanation just conjectured has the advantage of integrating Aristotle's restriction on L with the 'necessary-when' fallacy at 19a23-7. For the restriction, the fallacy and its solution all have a common source in the concept of RT-possibility whose application requires the suppositional method. But as an account of *De Interpretatione* 9 the explanation fails, because although Aristotle could scarcely have rejected the epistemic point its import is too wide to account for his special concern in that chapter. The determinist who holds that what will happen tomorrow has always been necessary may nevertheless try to predict the event from known facts, and in that case he *ipso facto* treats the truth or falsity of the proposition as not included among them. Or we may use the method of supposition to decide whether the known situation is consistent with 'There was a battle yesterday' and also with its negation, and epistemically the case is identical with that of their future-tensed counterparts. There can be no reason here for treating only future-tensed contingents as neither true nor false.[13]

A reason often suggested is that Aristotle takes '"p" is true at t' to imply that at t the world is *such* that 'p' is then true. Thus if 'p' says that E will occur later than t, its truth at t would entail that the actual situation then is already such as to ensure that E will occur. In Professor Ackrill's words:

He seems to hold a rather crude realistic correspondence theory of truth, and we might well expect him to think that if the state of affairs now is such that it is not settled whether X will or will not occur, then 'X will occur' is not now either true or false: there is not yet anything in the facts for it to correspond with or fail to correspond with.[14]

No doubt it is correct to say that Aristotle conceives of truth in terms of correspondence, and perhaps his conception is primitive. But on his own showing he does not interpret the truth–fact relationship in a way that compels him to sacrifice prior truth in the interest of contingency.

---

[13] As von Wright points out, op. cit. p. 244.

[14] Op. cit., pp. 140-1. (Ackrill does not decisively favour this view of Aristotle.) See also Cahn, Ch. 3, esp. pp. 41-2.

His word for the obtaining of that state of affairs which makes a statement true is 'ὑπάρχειν', which occurs several times with this meaning in *De Interpretatione* 9. On the view suggested, we should expect the tense of 'ὑπάρχειν' in any given instance to follow that of the second-order statement attributing truth. Thus if he says that '*p*' *is* true (whatever the tense of '*p*' itself), he ought to say that the corresponding state of things 'ὑπάρχει' (present tense). In fact his usage seems to follow a different rule. Even where he says that '*p*' *is* true he makes the tense of 'ὑπάρχειν' accord with that of '*p*' (see 18a35–8; b21–3). In other words, what "makes" '*p*' true, whenever it is true, is the obtaining of a certain state of affairs at just the time to which '*p*' by its date or tense assigns it; and this time does not necessarily coincide with that when '*p*' is true, since, for instance, a past-tensed '*p*' is true even when the situation it describes is over. Similarly Aristotle's phraseology suggests that a future-tensed '*p*' may now be true although what makes it so still lies ahead. The future obtaining of the future state of affairs is not only necessary but also sufficient for the present truth of '*p*'. At no point does Aristotle suggest that this sufficiency holds only via the mediation of a present state in which there somehow already obtains the future obtaining of what '*p*' says will occur.[15]

I have now discussed two sorts of consideration, one epistemic, the other ontological, that might drive a philosopher to suspend truth-values for future-tensed contingents. If, as I have argued, *De Interpretatione* 9 bears no traces of either of these pressures, are we thrown back on the *sensu diviso* interpretation of L, according to which Aristotle's

---

[15] For a similar point about past-tensed '*p*' see below, p. 120. Aristotle, I think, would have agreed with Mrs. Kneale (*The Development of Logic*, p. 51) that 'By introducing the phrase "it is true that" we make no assumption about determinism which is not made by the use of the simple sentence in the future tense.' See also C.J.F. Williams, 'True Tomorrow, Never True Today', *Phil. Quart.* 1978, pp. 285 ff. A variant of the view just considered in the text is that there is (or seems to be to Aristotle) a sense of 'is true' in which 'It is true at *t* that *p*' means 'It is settled or already determined at *t* that *p*' (see, e.g., von Wright, pp. 242–3). That Aristotle saw this as the *only* sense of 'is true' cannot be reconciled with 19a32–9. If on the other hand he also in *De Int.* 9 recognizes a sense in which '"*p*" is true' entails nothing stronger than '*p*', it is hardly credible that he should have been too confused to see that L on this meaning needs no restriction, or seeing it, so casual as to neglect to *say*: 'In one sense L applies universally, in another not'.

bugbear is not truth-value but only necessary truth-value? In the following section I shall maintain that on one point such an account is correct: in denying R for future contingents he does not deny them truth-value as such. But this is not because by L he means: 'For all pairs, one side is *necessarily* true and the other *necessarily* false'.

L on the natural reading is: 'for all antithetical pairs, necessarily one side is true and the other false'. So far we have studied this only in the context of Chapter 9. But if we look back to Chapters 7 and 8, we find Aristotle denying a proposition verbally identical with L. And as with L in 9, he does not deny outright its status as a principle, but only restricts its scope. In 7 and 8 he is not concerned with future-tensed statements, nor with contingency, and there the point of the restriction is that in some antithetical pairs, the two sides need not have the *opposite* values of truth and falsity. The idea that *neither* value is attributable at all to either side is irrelevant to the discussion of 7 and 8. But a consecutive reading of 7, 8 and 9 strongly suggests that in the third of these chapters Aristotle is extending to a new set of cases the very point established in the first and second. If this is so, then what he objects to in 9 is the idea of a necessary *opposition* of truth-values for future-tensed pairs. Why he should think that this would threaten contingency is a question to be considered. But before turning to that, let us see how the text supports the view that in 9 his point is essentially the same as in 7 and 8.

To follow his reasoning in 7 and 8 we have to be clear what he means by an *antithesis* (ἀντίφασις) or pair of *antithetical* (ἀντικείμενα) propositions. It consists of a single affirmation (κατάφασις) and a corresponding single denial (ἀπόφασις). If we take an "affirmation" to be a proposition considered without regard for its internal structure, then the "denial" of '*p*' would be its external negation, and it seems absurd even to raise the question whether in some cases the truth-values are not opposed. However, as Aristotle defines them, an "affirmation" affirms something *of* something, and a corresponding "denial" denies the same thing of the same thing (6, 17a25 ff.). And by 'thing' in its first occurrence he means a predicative term, while by the second occurrence he means an unquantified term, either a name or a general term considered in abstraction from quantifiers. Thus the following are antithetical pairs:

(1)   Socrates is white/Socrates is not white;
(2)   All men are white/All men are not white;
(3)   A man is white/A man is not white;
(4)   All men are white/Some man is not white. (See Chapter 7.)

Aristotle's inclusion of the third case shows clearly that the pairing relationship depends on the sameness of *terms* on either side, whether or not the subject-term in both covers the same *objects*. In 7 Aristotle shows how in (1) and (4), but not in (2) and (3), the sides must be one true, one false. In stating this he sometimes speaks of the necessity that one be true *and* the other false (17b30; cf. 18a26-7); and sometimes of the necessity that one *or* other be true *or* false (17b 27; cf. 18a10-12). It is clear that these locutions are equivalent; that is, that 'true *or* false' in the latter implies that one member has truth *by contrast with* the falsity of the other. Then in 8 he moves on to consider cases where one or both terms stand for two things which do not form a unity, as e.g. when the subject-term means both 'horse' and 'man' at the same time. "Pairs" constructed with these are not well-formed, since each side is either meaningless or consists of more than one affirmation and denial. Aristotle does not deal very systematically with these cases, but the upshot is that if the two sides mean anything, there is no necessity for opposite truth-values; not even when the antithesis is of form (4) above.[16] Presumably he would agree that if they are meaningless, neither has a truth-value at all. But this (which is not explicitly said) is no evidence for his entertaining the idea that in some *meaningful and well-formed* pairs (as for instance

[16] Both sides may be false. For, he says, if 'X' does duty for 'horse' and 'man' simultaneously, then 'An X is white', if it means anything, means 'A man is white and a horse is white'. Thus 'All X's are white' would mean 'All men are white and all horses are white'. This and its contradictory 'Some X is not white' (similarly construed) may both be false, e.g. if all men are white and some horses not. Cf. Ackrill pp. 130-2.

a single singular future-tensed statement and its contradictory) each side lacks both the standard truth-values.

Chapter 8 ends: 'Thus it is not necessary in these cases
either [*sc.* those of non-unitary terms] that one side of an
antithesis be true and the other false' (18a26–7). Chapter 9
straight away begins: 'With regard, then (οὖν), to things past
and present, it is necessary that either the affirmation or the
denial be true or false . . .' (now there follows a parenthesis)
'. . . but for singular propositions referring to the future it is
not the same' (18a28–34.) Ackrill[17] for one sees 'true or
false' here as meaning 'having one or other standard truth-
value', and holds that this is what Aristotle denies for both
sides of some future-tensed singular pairs. On this view, instead of continuing with his distinction between pairs with
and pairs without necessarily opposite values, Aristotle now
launches into a new distinction between pairs with and pairs
without (standard) truth-value at all. But how in thus changing
direction could he fail to signal the consequent shift in
meaning of 'true or false', which alluded first to an opposition of truth-value, and now (it is alleged) to the possession
of truth-value as such? How too, in that case, could he lead
into 9 with the connective 'οὖν' (= 'then', 'so')? It is true
that the opening sentence of 9 is not a strict consequence of
what precedes, since it broaches a subject not yet mentioned,
namely the significance of tenses. But at the very least 'οὖν'
indicates continuance of the same general line of thought.

This is borne out by the fact that in the parenthesis left
out of the last quotation Aristotle breaks off to summarize
the results already achieved in 7, and gives no indication that
these belong to a different topic. (Chapter 8 he ignores, since
it relates only to improper cases.) The parenthesis runs: 'And
with universals universally quantified one side is in all cases
true and the other false, and also with singulars, as has been
said; but for universals not universally quantified it is not
necessary, as has also been said.' On a reading such as Ackrill's,
the transition from 8 to 9 goes as follows: (a) 8 ends with the
denial of an *opposition* of values in certain cases; (b) 9 opens
with the assertion, for certain cases (past- and present-tensed),

[17] Op. cit. pp. 133–4.

that truth-value *as such* applies; almost at once (c) there is an allusion back to an earlier division of cases into those with and those without a necessary *opposition*; and then (d) Aristotle quickly returns to the question of truth-value *as such*, this time to mark off future-tensed singulars as lacking it. Perhaps it is not incredible that he should weave thus between two quite different distinctions; but what passes belief is that throughout he should use the same terms ('true or false' and the synonymous 'one true, the other false') to cover both in quick alternation. Ackrill contends that the context at the beginning of 9 'makes it clear' that in the body of that chapter Aristotle is concerned with a different point from the one in 7 and 8. But by 'context' here Ackrill can- not mean the verbal context, since on a natural reading this yields no trace of a difference. What he has in mind, I believe, is the logical context, i.e. the thrust of the subsequent argu- ment in 9. For prima facie it is impossible to make sense of this on the assumption that Aristotle's anxiety over con- tingency centres on the notion of *opposed* truth-value.

This problem cries out for attention, but before turning to it let me end this discussion of the opening of Chapter 9 by stating what I take to be the actual sequence of thought. In 7 and 8 no notice was taken of the tenses of antithetical pairs. Singular and general antitheses were compared in respect of the truth-values possible on either side, and amongst the general a relevant contrast was drawn by refer- ence to the presence or absence of a universal quantifier. Singular pairs were treated *en bloc* under the single illustra- tion 'Socrates is white'/'Socrates is not white'. If this example is typical of the whole class, it is clear that 'Necessarily one true, one false' applies to them all. Aristotle reminds us of this conclusion at the beginning of 9 (18a30–1). But he re- calls it here in order to modify it. For a division can also be made according to tense, and this not only cuts across the previous classification but raises the question of opposed truth-values from a new angle. And now the answer to this does not entirely coincide with the previous results. For when singulars are not all treated alike but divided by tense, it becomes apparent (so Aristotle holds) that one sub- division, that of future-tensed pairs, does not behave like the others. The reason, he is about to argue, is that these pairs, or some of them, represent contingencies, and contingency is incompatible with 'one true, one false'.

If Aristotle is not disturbed by truth-value as such of future contingents, why should he balk at their value-opposition? And as a rational man how could he? Unlike 'A man is white'/'A man is not white', the pair 'We shall fight tomorrow'/'We shall not fight tomorrow' are not merely antithetical but mutually exclusive. How then can truth-values be applied at all unless they are opposed as true to false? The text, it must be admitted, provides no clear answers. But after all no one imagines it possible to interpret *De Interpretatione* 9 without resort to conjecture.

By the end of the first section Aristotle takes himself to have made it clear that 'Necessarily, one true, one false' erases contingency. It is this sequence of thought we have to explain, also explaining, if possible, why he should have supposed it so much more lucid than it is. He first states it not, as we should say, in terms of antithetical propositions, but of opposed statements or assertions by which one person contradicts (whether knowingly or not we are not told) what is said by another. If things are as they are said to be, then the assertion is true and the man who makes it asserts truly ('ἀληθεύει'), while (if L is assumed) the man who asserts the antithetical asserts falsely ('ψεύδεται'; cf. 18a35–b8).

Consider a pair of future-tensed singular antitheticals each asserted in a situation where everyone concerned has reason to believe that the natural state of things independent of human agency does not determine an outcome one way or the other. The assertions can express various attitudes. (1) Either or both may express a sheer hunch. Or (2) either or both may express an agent's decision as to what will happen, i.e. what he will bring about. Or (3) either or both may express a prediction (by the agent himself or another) based on the knowledge that someone has decided one way or the other (made an assertion of type (2)).

Let us focus on the second case. When an agent says, deciding (not divining, guessing or predicting), that X will happen at *t*, is it reasonable to prohibit the application of the word 'True' to this utterance? This may make sense if what is meant is that no one is entitled to claim absolute certainty that things will be as the agent decides to make them. For even if nothing in the present situation is destined to prevent him, a contingent obstacle may newly arise (say in the shape of a human interfering agent who has not yet made up his mind to interfere), or the man himself may alter his decision. However, those who hold future contingents to be neither true nor false are maintaining not an epistemological but a logical position, according to which 'True' here has *no* application, not merely none that excludes all doubt. To them, 'Probably it is (now) true' is as ill-formed as 'Beyond doubt, it is . . .'. For their objection is to the phrase that lies within the scope of whichever epistemic operator.

This is a strange position. The mere fact that an agent asserts (in the mode of decision) 'X will occur at *t*' gives an external observer some reason (though not conclusive) to believe that the event will happen. For the decision-assertion is really the last step in practical reasoning and the first step in the action itself. Already the process has started, by the very fact of the assertion, and the observer has at least as much right to expect its completion as if he had perceived the beginnings of some natural process. In this case he takes himself to be to some extent justified in reading off what will happen from the agent's assertion that it will. Or we may say: the assertion alone provides a degree of entitlement to "take the asserter's word for it". By willing, the agent constitutes himself an authority or source of information on what will happen, even though it would be foolish to treat this authority as absolute. But that is not in general a reason why non-authorities (such as the observer in this case) should be forbidden to say that what the authority says is true. And in this case too it would, I suggest, have seemed perfectly natural to Aristotle to regard the agent as making what an observer is entitled to call a 'true' assertion about how things will be. An observer may not be entitled to call it 'true' with complete confidence. But we are concerned with *what* he would be justified in saying, not the degree of justification.

If the agent does not do as he willed, his decision-assertion turns out not to have been true. But this does not entail that earlier no one had the right to trust it. However, if two agents will incompatible ends the observer can hardly accept both assertions as truly representing what will happen. By the present account he has some right to this acceptance in each case, but his reason for taking one agent's word for it will *eo ipso* be a reason for rejecting the other's. The authorities clash, and if the observer is inclined (which he may not be) to follow one rather than the other, this will be because he estimates one as more able or more determined. However, the question is this: is it correct to say that the observer's reasons (however strong or weak) for ascribing truth to one assertion are *eo ipso* reasons for ascribing *falsity* to the other? Again it must be stressed that the question is not whether there are conclusive reasons in favour of either side. Clearly there are not in the situation described, since each side supplies the observer with some reason to trust it, hence not to trust the other. The point at issue is whether *to the extent* to which he is entitled to take either as true, and hence to reject the other, he is to that extent entitled to take the rejected one as false. And again, is he entitled to say of the one which later turns out to be unfulfilled that (although there was some reason to take it as true) it was in fact false?

If a modern analyst allows the initial assumption that there is no impropriety in ascribing 'true' in such cases, he is unlikely to deny that this ascription to either side entails a complementary 'false' for the other. For if 'false' is regarded simply as the value which attaches to the sentence or proposition '*p*' when 'true' attaches to 'not-*p*', and vice versa, there is no problem. But Aristotle is dealing not merely with propositions and sentences but with assertions and asserters. If an assertion is false ('ψευδής') the asserter (whose sincerity is here taken for granted) is to that extent involved in falsity: he ψεύδεται. But this word in Aristotle's natural Greek carries an overtone absent from the modern logician's pure semantic use of 'false'. The former suggests that the subject is deceived, in error, or mistaken. Thus if every assertion is assumed to be true or else false, Aristotle is committed to holding that if the man whose assertion expresses his will fails to bring the willed situation about, this is a sufficient condition for saying that the assertion was erroneous.

Does this make sense? It may of course be proper to say that the agent erred in respect of his assertion. For instance he may have been mistaken in thinking the goal desirable. But this is not to the point: our question concerns not the wisdom of his purpose but its fulfilment. Again, he may have been mistaken in his estimation that the future was not already determined one way or the other, or in his choice of means. Or he may have wrongly predicted that nothing would come up to make him change his mind, or no new contingency arise to interfere. Such predictions are not, however, a necessary feature of agency. The agent may not even consider those possibilities. And if he does he may well be disinclined to predict one way or the other. An open mind on this score does not imply practical suspense or vacillation. On the contrary: he may not envisage abandoning his purpose, or having it unforeseeably thwarted, unless he has a definite purpose to *be* abandoned or thwarted.

Suppose then a case where in an observer's opinion the agent avoids all these mistakes: i.e. he correctly judges the situation not to be predetermined, he adopts appropriate means, and does not make, hence does not erroneously make, the predictions mentioned above. It may still be that the willed outcome fails to occur. The question is whether this alone would entitle the observer retrospectively to regard the willing, or its expression, as a mistaken assertion, his sole ground being that it turned out to have been untrue. Again: if in advance the observer has some reason to expect non-fulfilment, is this by itself a reason for attributing error?

The man who states: 'I am making a statement' cannot be mistaken in this. With certain qualifications the agent's assertion of will resembles this case, and to that extent is infallible. Even when his will-assertion turns out not to have been true, to have made it was scarcely a mistake when the very asserting increased the chances of truth. There is a difference between this and 'I am making a statement', because in the latter the stating is identical with the act in virtue of which what is said is true. Whereas the agent's assertion that X will occur is true only if he manages to complete the action or series of actions that brings X about, and in general this process is still incomplete when the assertion has already been made. That is why the process can be broken off and the assertion turn out untrue. But even when incomplete it was on the way to completion, and since the assertion was responsible for the process as far as it went, it would be absurd to call it erroneous, whatever the outcome. For the assertion of will does not simply start the process as if this then unrolled under its own momentum, but is in some sense maintained continuously, since the process goes on in the light of the willed end. From the start it is true to say that the agent has willed or asserted, but this does not imply that the assertion is over from the start. It continues present, not because it needs time itself to develop but because the process does, and as long as *this* is incomplete it must be willed to continue.

So in the case where the agent carries out what he wills, the situation closely parallels that of the man who says 'I am making a statement'. The stating of this is not over before the performance of the action responsible for the truth of what is stated: for the stating *is* the action. Similarly, the fully effective agent's assertion is not over before the performance of the action responsible for its truth. However, effectiveness is not guaranteed, which is why the action and the assertion cannot be said to be identical. 'I am making a statement' is self-fulfilling whatever the circumstances. But there are circumstances when the agent still asserts, but the assertion is not self-fulfilling: as when an insurmountable obstacle arises which he has not yet recognized as such. Or he may continue willing even having brought matters to a point from which the desired result is inevitable by natural law. Either way the asserting is now vain. In one case the future result is now impossible, in the other now necessary. But as long as it was still contingent, the assertion was effective in bringing itself towards fulfilment. So whatever the final outcome, there was never a time when the will-assertion was both contingent and properly to be described as 'false' (except in the purely semantic sense). For suppose that the outcome fails to occur because the agent abandons his purpose halfway. Then the original assertion was not after all true. But nor was it ever a falsehood. For as long as the agent continued to act the assertion was making itself true;

and although this ceases to be the case once he gives up, the assertion too has ceased. It is not now the agent's error because he no longer makes it, and when he did make it he was not in error either.

So where different agents make conflicting assertions each of which corresponds to a possible situation, then although in each case there is some ground for ascribing truth, this is not a ground for calling the other 'false' if this word and its Greek equivalents are used with their natural·language connotations. If anyone insists that in all contradictory pairs there has to be one side true and the other false, then in the eyes of one who takes 'false' in its unsophisticated sense, that person in effect denies contingency. For he implies that the mere non-occurrence of an event is sufficient grounds for ascribing prior falsity to any future-tensed assertion of it; which in turn implies that no such assertion would have been even partially self-fulfilling: but this would be true only if prior to the assertion the event was necessary or impossible in advance.

This, I suggest, is the rationale of *De Interpretatione* 9. It might have been obvious to us if Aristotle had explained that he uses 'false' in the naive sense. But it would be *naiveté* on our part to expect him to have anticipated the bafflement of later critics who bring to the text the assumption that 'false' is there used with the denaturalized quasi-technical meaning of contemporary logic.

Since the above argument is perfectly general it follows that if every assertion is false unless true, then however long beforehand someone asserts something about the future, 'even ten thousand years' (18b33-6), the event is already settled. Whenever an agent's assertion occurs or might have occurred, it would always come too late to find matters still contingent, i.e. as capable of being influenced one way or another by the very assertion itself of how they will go. Aristotle draws the consequence that 'There would be no need to take trouble about practical affairs or deliberate' (18b31-3). Here he says that if L holds unrestrictedly, deliberations and decisions would not affect what happens. Apparently it does not occur to him that a determinist might treat these too as predetermined links in causal chains issuing in actions and other consequences. In that case it would not be true that they make no difference; only that the difference they make was just as settled ten thousand years before the inevitable decision as at any time afterwards. However, Aristotle's failure to explore this form of determinism does not materially affect his main conclusion, which is that we cannot rationally maintain L without restriction, understanding its implications, and also engage sometimes in decision and deliberation. For in deciding we take it that different outcomes and different decisions were possible, and when we deliberate it is because we believe that otherwise we risk making a worse decision when a better is available. Since decision and deliberation logically presuppose these assumptions, if we are predetermined to engage in the former we are also predetermined to accept the latter, at the time at least. So as a creature who sometimes decides, I am sometimes logically bound to reject the unrestricted L, if I understand what it entails. However strong my reasons for maintaining it when I do, my adherence can be no more than intermittent at best, and if I maintain it at all I must confess myself irrational in respect of this principle, since I also abandon it, not because I have new reason to suppose it false, but because sometimes I cannot help deciding something. To a philosopher like Hume such a situation is not conceptually repugnant, but Aristotle would surely maintain that man's rational nature cannot be at odds with his practical and deliberative side, since this itself is subject to reason. Hence as *rational* agents we must reject for good a principle which as *agents* we cannot consistently maintain.

Since we cannot rationally view decision as predetermined even if it is, we must accept its nature at face value, i.e. as capable of going either way. In that case we see decisions as points of origin for actions and their consequences, as causes but not effects. On that premiss Aristotle is correct in holding that in a universe devoid of contingency no decision would make a difference. For if decision itself were even possible nothing would depend on it, since for every decision that is or might be made it is already settled what will happen, and decision is not a link in the chain. Thus in drawing out the absurd consequences of the unrestricted L Aristotle says:

There is no reason why someone should not assert and someone else deny that such and such will happen ten thousand years ahead: which implies [given L] that there will later occur of necessity whichever event it was then true to say would happen. What is more, it does not even make any difference whether the affirmation and denial were asserted by anyone or not. For it is clear that this is how things are [i.e. they are now such that the outcome will be as it will be], even if one person does not affirm and the other deny. For it is not because of the affirming or denying that the event will be or not be; this is equally true whatever the temporal interval, even if it is ten thousand years. (18b33–19a1.)

Here he is generally understood to be saying that the unrestricted R does away with all contingency, not merely the contingency of events corresponding to true assertions actually made. That follows; for if the future-tensed '*p*' asserted now is now true-as-opposed-to-false and hence now necessary, this can only be because the situation now is such as to necessitate the outcome, and that would still have been so even if '*p*' had not been asserted. I take this to be a part of Aristotle's meaning, but he is, I think, implying not only that the necessity does not depend on any actual assertion, but also that the event itself does not. In other words: despite the apparent power of so-called agents' assertions to bring things about, everything in fact goes on exactly as if these were never made.

If it is not *truth* that Aristotle refuses to ascribe to a certain class of statements, but *truth-as-opposed-to-falsity*, his adherence to the unrestricted Law of Excluded Middle presents no paradox. The connection between 'Either *p* or not-*p*' and 'Either it is true that *p* or it is true that not-*p*' remains intact for all '*p*'. Nor is there any reason why, when '*p*' refers to the future, he should not say that either it or its contradictory has always been true (i.e. would have been the gist of a true assertion made however far back). To say that '*p*' was always true is not to say that things were always such that '*p*' had to be true;[18] the latter does not follow unless the truth of '*p*' is taken to entail the falsity of 'not-*p*'.

But in rejecting falsity for one side of a contradictory pair while allowing truth for the other, what status does Aristotle give to the first? In cases such as we have been considering

[18] See above, pp. 93 f.

both sides are singular and refer to the same particular event; hence they are not like the antithesis 'A man is white'/'A man is not white', where both states of affairs can hold simultaneously (cf. 18a35-9). It is true that if 'X will occur at *t*' and 'X will not occur at *t*' are each of them agent-assertions both can for a time be self-fulfilling; but only one can win through to completion. Hence each so to speak approximates to truth, but only one turns out to *have* it, since (as Aristotle elsewhere[19] says) it is true now that X will be, only if it is true later that it is.

Hence some assertions are not true and not false. Aristotle suggests no label for this status. It cannot be put down as 'intermediate' between truth and falsity, since that would imply that these are both possible alternatives. The non-truth of an agent's contingent assertion (when not fulfilled) is as much opposed to the truth of whatever contradicts it as falsity is to truth in past- and present-tensed pairs. Aristotle's curious position does not really break with the Principle of Bivalence. For every assertion there are just two values possible: only in some cases the second value is not 'false' but 'not true'. What Aristotle needs here is the purely semantic concept of falsity; except that had he possessed it the problem of *De Interpretatione* 9 would not have arisen.

He himself does not always find it easy to stop saying 'false' whenever he means 'not true'. When arguing near the end against the fallacy of division performed on the Law of Excluded Middle he says this about contradictory pairs of contingents:

In these cases it is necessary that one side of the antithetical pair *be true or false* [i.e. *true-as-opposed-to-false*], but not that it be this particular side or that; only that it be one or the other, whichever way it chances; and it is necessary, rather (μᾶλλον), that one side be true [or: it is necessary that one side be more true], *but not on that account* (οὐκ ἤδη) [or: *not already*] *true or* [i.e. *as-opposed-to*] *false*. Hence it is clear that it is not necessary that in all antithetical affirmations and denials one side is true and one false. (19a36-b4.)

So ends the chapter. On any interpretation there is a discrepancy between the italicized phrases, showing the writer's

---

[19] *De Gen. et Corr.* II.11, 337b3-7, where he points out that 'X is on the way to happening' does not entail 'X will happen'.

difficulty in adjusting his terminology to an odd conclusion, and the oddity clearly has something to do with truth-value. As I read it, he is caught momentarily by the logician's cliché 'true-as-opposed-to-false'[20] but then (since he is speaking of contingents) quickly corrects himself, substituting: 'True, but not true-as-opposed-to-false'. This general interpretation fits in with each of the various possible translations. If '$\mu\hat{\alpha}\lambda\lambda o\nu$' governs the whole subsequent clause it explicitly signals his self-correction. If it goes with '$\dot{\alpha}\lambda\eta\theta\hat{\eta}$', then he is recommending that we think of contingent contradictories as 'one more, one less true', which is a way of refusing to say that either is false.[21] If this is his meaning, the comparison is not, I think, between degrees of likelihood,[22] but refers to the fact that an unfulfilled agent-assertion goes *some* way towards getting itself fulfilled (if, that is, it ever was contingent in the first place). In saying this he must not be taken to imply that the less true is more false. As for the notorious '$\H{\eta}\delta\eta$', it may have either the logical[23] or the chronological meaning. The point of the former (which denies an apparent implication, i.e. = 'that is not to say that') is that normally 'true' would be understood as 'true-as-opposed-to-false'. If the chronological sense is meant, his point would be that when an assertion's date lies still in the future, it is not yet true-as-opposed-to-false, but will be once the date is present.

On this account, the fallacies discussed in the third section are not quite so closely tied to L as they would be if, as some think, L were the explicit disjunction of necessities reached by means of those fallacies. But L as I understand it does entail that disjunction for all assertions to which it applies. Now as Aristotle's own words show in the passage last quoted, it is not easy to curb the impulse to propound L for all genuinely contradictory pairs, even if one is aware of the consequences for contingency. And if independent logic seems to lead to

---

[20] Probably because his point about fallacious division is a general one, and where 'p' is in a past or present tense it would be proper to say 'Necessarily, either "p" or "not-p" is true-as-opposed-to-false (but it does not follow that necessarily one rather than the other)'.

[21] For 'more or less true' cf. *Metaph*. Γ.4, 1008b5 ff. and 31 ff.

[22] Since it is not necessary that one or other be more probable.

[23] Suggested by G.E.M. Anscombe, 'Aristotle and the Sea Battle', *Mind* LXV, 1956.

the same result the impulse will look like a sound instinct, and the loss of contingency becomes simply something to be endured. This is why Aristotle takes care to show that the logic is spurious.

So the argument of *De Interpretatione* 9 turns, if I am right, on two asymmetries, one celebrated, the other obscure. By the first, contingency belongs only with the future tense; by the second it is consistent with prior truth but not prior falsity. The first follows from the fundamentally temporal character of Aristotle's modalities, while the second results entirely from a use of 'false' in which the natural connotations are as yet not refined out. The modal asymmetry of tense tends to support the asymmetry of truth-value. In a system of non-temporalized modal concepts in which '*p/t*' can at any time be contingent, there is no unique relation of contingency with the field of possible agency; nor therefore with practical assertions that are infallible to the extent that they are self-fulfilling. Many assertions will be contingent that are also false in Aristotle's rich sense, and so there will be no appearance of general incompatibility between these two concepts.

But if Aristotle's temporalized approach to modality reinforces his naive refusal to apply 'false' to contingents, the two positions are all the same logically independent. Held in conjunction they generate the logical problem of *De Interpretatione* 9, and Aristotle's lack of self-consciousness about the second is responsible for the obscurity of presentation. But in itself the use of 'false' to imply 'mistaken' entails no special commitment to RT-modality, while RT-modality as such requires no stronger meaning for 'false' than the semantic.

VI

Change and contingency

The object of this study was to identify Aristotle's grounds for holding (A') that what is possible is at some time realized, and (B') that what always is, is of necessity. One view locates the source of these doctrines in the very meaning he gives to the modal terms themselves, claiming that he understands them or their rule of use in such a way that A' and B' directly result as analytic propositions. The preceding four chapters form a cumulative argument against ascribing to Aristotle so outlandish a conception of modality. I have shown that his formal remarks about possibility in *De Caelo* I.12 point to an intelligible relative notion which by itself is incapable of generating A' and B'. This also occurs in *De Interpretatione* 9. The arguments and conclusions of both these passages are strange by our standards, but they can be explained without postulating bizarre modal concepts. In particular, A' and B' in *De Caelo* depend on extraneous metaphysical assumptions. However, these assumptions do not fully account for the tenacity with which Aristotle maintains B', at least in some form; for at some stage he rejected the conception of infinity used in the *De Caelo* argument, and it is not clear what alternative provision was made. Until this question is resolved there will still be some ground for doubting whether it is not some latent quirk in his approach to modality as such that assures him of B' even without the aid of all the *De Caelo* premisses. This doubt will be met in the next chapter by an argument showing that A' and B' (or versions of them) are entailed by the metaphysical principles governing change and becoming in a universe of Aristotelian substances. But it is necessary first to clarify the connection between Aristotelian possibility and change.

In a changeless and timeless (or "instantaneous") universe the state of things might still be logically contingent in the absolute sense which demands only that the alternative entail no self-contradiction. Even in a temporal world, moreover, contingency in this sense may be spelt out without allusion to change. For 'p' is contingent if and only if 'not-p' is self-consistent, whether or not 'p' and 'not-p' represent *termini* of a possible intervening change. For instance, if 'p' is the dated proposition 'Fa/t_n' there can be no change from the state of affairs represented by this to the one represented by its negation '$\sim Fa/t_n$' or vice versa. Now it may be that as well as the truth of 'Fa/t_n' we have also the truth of '$\sim Fa/t_o$' where $o \neq n$. In that case there is change through time between the situations represented by the undated 'Fa' and '$\sim Fa$' (understood as in the present tense). But the absolute logical contingency of 'Fa/t_n' does not depend on this fact and can be decided without reference to it or to its possibility. We need only know that '$\sim Fa/t_n$' is self-consistent; and if this is so, it is so whether or not '$\sim Fa/t_o$' is or might be true as well.

For Aristotle on the other hand, the contingency of 'Fa/t_n' depends not on its relation, viz. that of contradicting, to *one* other (self-consistent) proposition, but on its relation to *two* others. 'Fa/t_n' is RT-contingent if and only if it and its contradictory are each consistent with a third. The third is a proposition 'q/t_m' where t_m is understood to be prior to t_n, and 'q' represents the state of things at t_m. Now at t_m either the undated present-tensed 'Fa' was true, or its contradictory was. So 'q/t_m' either includes 'Fa/t_m' or it includes '$\sim Fa/t_m$'. Let it include the former. Then 'q/t_m' is consistent with both 'Fa/t_n' and '$\sim Fa/t_n$' only if the truth of 'Fa' at t_m is consistent with its falsity at t_n: in other words, only if there is no inconsistency in supposing that the situation at t_m represented by 'Fa' gives way to a situation represented by '$\sim Fa$'. Similarly if 'q/t_m' includes '$\sim Fa/t_m$'. In this case the contingency of 'Fa/t_n' depends on the possibility that $\sim Fa$ should give way to Fa. The dated propositions cannot change in truth-value. But their contingency depends on the possibility of change in truth-value of related dateless ones. Just so, if we consider facts rather than propositions, it is an eternal fact that Fa/t_n (if 'Fa/t_n' is true), but the contingency of this depends on the possibility of actual change from the state of things depicted by 'Fa' to that depicted by '$\sim Fa$', or vice versa.

This conclusion, that for Aristotle the contingency of something's *being* F/not-F depends on the prior possibility of its *becoming* F/not-F, sets the direction for the rest of this chapter. It is this connection with change that explains the temporal asymmetry of his modal concepts. It also, I shall argue, implies that for him possibilities and necessities belong primarily not on the level of propositions or their linguistic expressions, but in the extra-linguistic world. For this reason the range of possibilities is limited by the fundamental conditions for natural change among natural substances. It is this that further accounts for the doctrines A' and B'. But before proceeding we must establish more firmly the conclusion just stated. For it may be granted that Aristotelian contingent being *entails* the possibility of change according to the above argument; but this is not yet to say that contingency of being *depends* on the possibility of change, as if on something more basic or fundamental. That would imply that a pair of propositions constant in truth-value, such as 'Fa/t_m' and '$\sim Fa/t_n$' are both true *because* the undated 'Fa' changes from true to false; and that the corresponding pair of eternal facts Fa/t_m and $\sim Fa/t_n$ obtains *because* the object called 'a' was F and has ceased to be so. But the logical relation set forth above between a certain combination of changeless items on the one hand, and change on the other, is consistent with a reversed order of explanation that would make the changeless ontologically prior to change.

In other words, it might be maintained that the basic facts of the universe (and on the side of language the basic sentences) incorporate a definite time-relation as a constituent. Such facts and sentences cannot change. When we speak of a change from Fa to not-Fa, we deal only with certain abstracted aspects of the basic facts. 'Fa' expresses a non-isolable component of the complex expressed by 'Fa/t_n' which the latter has in common with complexes expressed by 'Fa/t_m', and 'Fa/t_o', etc. 'Fa' stands for something like a universal, with no self-sufficient existence. John's walking is not a reality independent of particular facts such as that John walks at t_n, any more than it is independent of facts such as that he walks fast in the direction of the police station.

Whoever walks does so somehow, somewhere, at some time, as Aristotle himself would agree. Therefore the "replacement" of the situation described by 'Fa' with that described by '~Fa' is only a relation between abstractions and has no more fundamental reality than they. This is not to say that change is unreal in the sense that propositions about change are meaningless or never true: only that it is not ultimately real, since the truth of such propositions depends on the metaphysically prior truth of dated changeless ones.

It needs no saying that this is not Aristotle's position: that for him, change is fundamental. Accordingly, although he recognizes the possibility of constructing dated sentences eternally true or false, his basic sentences are dateless ones in the present tense whose truth-value can vary (see in particular *Categories* 5, 4a23 ff.). Hintikka has devoted a chapter[1] to exploring the presuppositions and consequences of this view of truth as held by Aristotle and other Greek philosophers. However, it is also worth raising the question whether this stand is reasonable compared with the opposite position sketched above. This is a large topic, and I shall confine myself to three points.

In the first place, according to Aristotle a "now", i.e. a sometime present moment of time, is necessarily one of many. A situation is *present* only if followed by another present from which the former is seen as past, and which itself was future as from then. He also argues that we perceive the difference of different "nows" only in so far as there is change. "Before and after" are seen as such only if the "nows" are experienced with different contents. The contents, therefore, cannot differ solely in respect of time. Hence they differ as fair from dark, large from small, etc.: i.e. there is change.[2] Thus the very temporality of a state of affairs, let alone any particular date it may be assigned, is at any rate epistemologically posterior to the experience of change and to changing experience. It follows that whether or not time itself is objectively real,[3] time presupposes change in reality as we know it.

---

[1] Hintikka, pp. 62 ff.   [2] *Physics* IV.11.

[3] As Aristotle defines it, there is time only in so far as the stages of change are counted and measured by rational beings. *Physics* IV.14, 223a21 ff.

Secondly, the metaphysics of non-change considered above owes its attraction in part to a certain view of the principal function of language: that it is for the conveying of information. However, 'conveying information' may be taken in different ways. Often it has been assumed that the ideal language is that which best expresses scientific knowledge. Scientific statements are intended to make available the same information to everyone everywhere and at any time, so that there may be a common stock on which any observation or hypothesis, with whomsoever it originates, can in principle be seen by all as having the same logical bearing, either for confirmation or the reverse. The scientific enterprise, being concerned with *'quod semper, quod ubique, quod ab omnibus'*, necessarily presupposes an immense disproportion between the number (indefinitely large) of those for whom the statements are intended, and the number of those to whom any particular statement's context of origin is accessible through the senses. Thus the question whether one contradicts another cannot be left to the context to determine, as for instance in the case of 'John is sitting', 'John is not sitting', which do not logically conflict if said at different times. Again, even if such ambiguities could be eliminated without dating the sentence, there is also the fact that the *scientific* value of a phenomenon is the same whenever it occurs. That is, its time does not affect its relevance or irrelevance to theory, whether the theory is current, obsolete or as yet unborn. What more natural than to register this constancy of relevance by casting the reports of phenomena in a form whose *truth*-value too must be constant: i.e. in dated tenseless form? Once it is assumed that the sentences primarily correct for the scientific purpose are primarily correct *simpliciter*, we easily arrive at the view that the metaphysically basic facts are dated ones.

Against this we may briefly argue as follows. Even if it is granted that language has one main function, and that this is the communicating of information, nothing has been said to show that the information's practical as opposed to theoretical value might not be what sets (or ought to set) the standard for rating one form of sentence more basic than another. From a practical point of view, the most effective (hence

primary) type of sentence will certainly be tensed, since for
practical purposes it makes all the difference whether for
instance the enemy's attack is past, present or future.[4] Since
the date alone does not tell us which, a date is useless without a tense, and with one often unnecessary. Those to whom
I issue information for practical purposes are generally those
whose behaviour can affect and be affected by my own: in
other words, they are generally my neighbours both spatially
and temporally speaking. Thus the utterer's "now" can frequently be assumed by both sides to be identical with the
recipient's, so that if I say in the present tense: 'John is
sitting', the interlocutor who tells me that John is not sitting
automatically knows and gives me to know, without benefit
of dates, that his statement contradicts mine. And practical
considerations apart, it may also be said that a sentence of
changeable truth-value is truer to the *experience* it describes
(hence is more expressive if not more informative) than those
dated counterparts by means of which science puts phenomena into cold storage for omnitemporal intellectual con-
sumption. For we do not experience dates as such, and could
not even think them were it not for awareness of change.[5]

Finally, there is the potentially misleading analogy between
'John is clever', '— is clever' on the one hand, and 'John is
sitting at t_n', 'John is sitting', on the other. The pairs are
similar in that the second member of each has an indeter-
minate truth-value by comparison with the first.[6] It may also
be thought that the first members are alike in more effectively
picturing a concrete situation which actually exists. This is
true in the case of the former pair. There is no actual state of
things corresponding to '— is clever' over and above the
cleverness of John, or of Mary, Jim, etc.. Still less (except for

---

[4] Cf. A.N. Prior, 'Thank Goodness That's Over!' (penultimate para.), *Philosophy* 34, 1959, pp. 12-17.

[5] On the epistemological priority of undated tensed sentences, see Prior ibid.,
and P.T. Geach, 'Some Problems about Time', British Academy lecture 1965, re-
printed in *Studies in the Philosophy of Thought and Action*, ed. Strawson,
Oxford 1967.

[6] Cf. Prior, *Past, Present and Future*, Oxford 1967, pp. 15 f.; J. White, 'Aristotle and Temporally Relative Modalities', *Analysis* 1979, pp. 88 ff., who calls
temporally indefinite propositions 'really propositional functions'; von Wright,
op. cit., p. 241.

the Platonist) is there such a state that is real *rather* than its particular instances. Hence it may seem that in general the more determinate a form of words, the more closely it corresponds to some concrete situation, so that given a more determinate set of propositions D_1, D_2, D_3, etc., and a less determinate set I_1, I_2, I_3, etc., we are entitled to assume that the world itself contains a set of concrete situations corresponding to each of the former, rather than a set corresponding to the latter. Thus it may come to look as if the more basic facts are changless dated ones. But this argument rests on a confusion of senses of 'determinate'. One proposition is more determinate than another if it conveys more information (can answer more questions without reference to the context of utterance). On the other hand, it is not necessarily more determinate in the sense of portraying something metaphysically more concrete. 'p' gives less information than 'It is a matter of contingent fact that p', yet few would be moved on this account to assert that there is a concrete situation, namely the contingent being of p, from which 'p' itself expresses only an abstraction. Again, 'p and q' is more informative than 'p', but not many of the philosophers who assume the priority of dated over undated sentences would allow that the "molecular" fact is more basic than its "atomic" components. And indeed, the above reasoning, if pursued, can only lead to the type of monism that identifies the one concrete fact with the entire universe, and the only truly accurate portrait of any state of affairs with an infinite proposition specifying its relations to every other.

Hence, returning to Aristotle, we have no need to apologize for his assumption that change and changeable actualities are fundamentally real, and that even though dated propositions are always true or always false, we only require dates (when we do) *because* things change, and not because reality cannot be faithfully represented except as changeless. And now the question arises: given that contingency of being presupposes the possibility of change, with change on *what level* is this contingency primarily associated? For change in the properties of things is paralleled by change in the truth-values of temporally indefinite propositions. This question leads to another which cannot be answered independently: are contingency and its contraries primarily properties of things or states of affairs in the world, or of propositions about them? Is a supposition possibly true because the corresponding situation is possible; or is the situation said to be possible only because the proposition is possibly true? And another associated question is this: is the possibility primarily relative to the *truth of a proposition* describing the actual situation, or to *the situation* itself?

The texts are of little help. In his use of modal terms Aristotle glides to and fro between the material and formal modes of discourse, as we saw in connection with *De Caelo* I.12.[7] The obvious equivalence of 'Necessarily Fa' with ' "Fa" is necessary', etc., entitle him to this passage, but his uninhibited use of it leaves the question of priority irritatingly open. He undoubtedly takes truth, and therefore change in truth-value, to be posterior to actuality and change in the world.[8] But this does not decisively commit him to locating contingency on one level rather than the other. Both the contingency of a situation and the contingent truth of the corresponding proposition depend ultimately on change in the world: this much is beyond question. But it could still be that 'contingent', and the other modal terms, apply primarily to propositions, and only then to the corresponding realities.

Professor Hintikka writes as if the difference of level is immaterial. In his chapter 'The Once and Future Sea Fight' he declares:

. . . everything that has been said in terms of truth in the course of this chapter could have been said in terms of being while keeping within the purview of genuinely Aristotelian ideas. (p. 168.)

And he preserves what he regards as a harmless ambiguity by using 'p' and 'q', etc. as stand-ins indifferently for sentences describing states of affairs and for designations of sentences. I shall argue that on the contrary it is not a matter of indifference: despite Aristotle's own lack of concern, his doctrines make sense only if his modalities belong primarily on the level of being.

[7] See above, pp. 28 ff.
[8] Cf. for instance *Cat.* 5, 4b6–10, discussed below.

But first let us consider Hintikka's position in more detail. He supports the remark just quoted by reference to Aristotle's attention in *De Interpretatione* 9 to the modal parallelism between being and truth. There are necessary and contingent states of affairs, and these are matched by λόγοι which are necessarily and contingently true (19a27 ff.). The correspondence does not in itself entail that neither level is modally prior to the other, but Hintikka overlooks this point. He not only issues the quoted statement without hint of qualification, but gives it the greatest emphasis. Alluding to a suggestion to the effect that in analysing Aristotelian modality it is important to differentiate being and truth, he says: 'It is hard to think of a suggestion that is more blatantly beside the point'; and a few lines later, after the reference to *De Interpretatione* 19a27 ff., we read: 'Thus any criticism [*sc.* of his own account] that turns on the contrast between being and truth . . . is without a shadow of substance.' (pp. 168-9.) It is fair, I think, to take Hintikka as ruling that the contrast is in every way irrelevant for a correct understanding of Aristotelian modality.

But in practice he is unable to maintain this stance. There are some cases in which he himself is committed to treating one level—the linguistic or propositional—as modally prior. To explain this let me recall the central position developed in Chapters V and VIII of *Time and Necessity*. This is that Aristotle, in holding A′ and B′, accepts a direct inference from 'possible' to 'at some time', and from 'always' to 'necessarily'. Hintikka even sees him as virtually committed to defining the modal by the temporal operators, although he readily admits that Aristotle does not state this openly and would not have entirely welcomed the idea. But reluctant though he may have been to accept the full implications, he cannot, in Hintikka's view, resist the pull to infer from omnitemporality as such to necessity.

It is the same with truth as with being, Hintikka believes. What always is, necessarily is, and what is always true is true necessarily. The aether is always, hence necessarily, in motion. The proposition 'The aether is in motion' is always, and so (by exactly the same principle) necessarily, true. But true dated propositions are also always true. Hence according to

Hintikka they too should count as necessary, even if what they refer to is a transient event, as e.g. 'John is sitting at t_n'. Hintikka does not distinguish as we have done between necessity-at-a-particular-time, and necessity-at-all-times. Hence he does not contrast the necessity at t_n of John's sitting at t_n (given that he does sit then) with the contingency prior to t_n of John's sitting at t_n; nor does Hintikka contrast this sort of case with a dated proposition such as 'The aether is in motion at t_n', which for Aristotle is not only always true but also always necessary.[9] Hintikka thinks that Aristotle is logically committed to treating all these always-true propositions as necessary in the same way and without reservation, the necessity being grounded simply on the fact that they are always true.[10]

True propositions in the past and future tenses referring to some particular event are not true always, but (respectively) for ever *after* and for ever *before* the event. But in each case we have truth for an infinity of time, although the infinity is in only one direction. In Hintikka's view, the inference from 'always' to 'necessarily' holds in these cases too,[11] so that a true future-tensed proposition which has been true *from* always was necessary in advance of the event. Accordingly, he proposes a novel account of Aristotle's dilemma in *De Interpretatione* 9. Rejecting the most usual interpretation, he writes:

Aristotle's problem was not primarily due to the apparent difficulties involved in the application of *tertium non datur* to statements about future events. It was generated rather by the fact that statements about

---

[9] Since there has never been a time when it was possible that the aether should ever cease rotating. I suppose that Aristotle would derive this from the presumed fact that it always does rotate. If he relies here on the *De Caelo* argument for B′, he is not quite justified, since motion and its species are not properties in any of the categories; cf. above, pp. 61 ff.

[10] Other objections apart, Hintikka's view would have to be qualified to accommodate the fact that in *Physics* VIII.6 and *Metaph.* Λ. 6 Aristotle evidently does not treat (a) 'It is always true that there is motion' (established in *Physics* VIII.1) as automatically entailing (b) 'Necessarily there is motion'. For in order to prove (b) he further has to argue that an endless succession of finite motions (which would verify (a)) has a *single* continuously operative cause.

[11] Despite Aristotle's indication at *De Caelo* I.12, 283a4–10, that the one-way infinite and the two-way infinite are logically very different. See above, p. 70.

future events have *always* been true if they are true at all, and *always* false if false at all. Statements of this kind were thought of by Aristotle as being true or false *necessarily*. (pp. 152–3.)

This approach is appealing prima facie because it seems to explain very neatly the Aristotelian doctrine that the past is necessary. For if something happened it is always thereafter true that it did. But it is in this particular application, i.e. to past-tensed statements, that we can see most clearly how Hintikka is in fact sometimes committed to assigning necessity to the statement or proposition rather than to the extra-linguistic state of affairs. He holds that the necessity is grounded in 'always'. But when an event is over, say Caesar's crossing the Rubicon, the only relevant subject to which 'always' can apply is the truth of the corresponding past-tensed statement. Aristotle (whose sense of reality was "robust") does not postulate actual extra-linguistic ever-lasting entities that match and confer truth upon past-tensed statements. There is no such currently actual situation as one consisting in Caesar's having crossed the Rubicon. It is a fact that he did, but to say that it *is* a fact is simply to say that 'Caesar crossed the Rubicon' is true. And it is true because something happened which is now over, namely his crossing. This to Aristotle is all we need say to explain the present truths of history.[12] Someone might retort that all the same the event, though itself now over, had natural effects whose train continues and will never be exhausted. But it is not the infinite series of effects that makes the past-tensed statement now true, but the original event. In this sort of case the only locus for 'always' is the truth about the past. Thus by Hintikka's account it is to this truth that necessity primarily belongs. The event itself is of course correctly classified as now necessary, but only because the statement is necessarily true, not vice versa. And if we were to tidy other cases into line with this, we should have to say that the necessity of the aether's everlasting motion is not primarily a feature of the cosmos or the aether or its motion, but derives from the fact that 'The aether is in motion' is always,

---

[12] Cf. pp. 93 f.

hence necessarily, *true*. Although truth itself depends on being, the *modality* of being depends on that of truth.

This is at odds with *De Caelo* I.12, where Aristotle is clearly concerned with the necessity of omnitemporal being, not truth. The argument there can of course be extended to prove that if it is always true that X is F then the same is also necessarily true; but this would be posterior to the conclusion relating to being, which depends on premisses that make no sense on the level of truth. Propositions or statements cannot be said to exercise organically conceived maximum-related capacities for being true or false. However, as we have seen,[13] the *De Caelo* reasons for B' may not be Aristotle's only reasons, so that Hintikka's interpretation of the 'always'/ 'necessarily' connection is not to be simply dismissed. It is still possible that Aristotle sometimes maintained it in the unmediated form which Hintikka envisages. And if so it would make sense for him to have maintained it on both levels indifferently, and without systematically making one of them prior. For if the connection depends only on the concepts 'always' and 'necessarily', and if their meaning in first-order and second-order contexts is essentially the same, then on either level the connection can occur in its own right.[14]

If *De Caelo* I.12 does not count against Hintikka's view, does *De Interpretatione* 9 support it? He himself sees it as providing the hitherto missing clue to that chapter. Aristotle's problem there, he holds, is to reconcile the contingency of 'There will be a sea-battle tomorrow' with the principle that 'always' directly entails 'necessarily'. The difficulty according to Hintikka arises because the statement if true or false in advance has always been true or false, so is (in advance) either necessarily true or necessarily false. Now as Hintikka sees it, Aristotle reacts not by denying truth-values for such

---

[13] P. 110; cf. 75 ff.

[14] Just as the inference from 'There are three so and so's' to 'There is more than one so and so' has the same rationale whether for 'so and so's' we substitute 'animals' or 'propositions'. However it is doubtful whether Aristotle would have thought that a λόγος is always true in the sense of 'always' in which, say, the aether always exists or rotates. The latter implies continuity, whereas 'always true' need only mean 'is true whenever thought or uttered'. The only candidates for being "continuously true" are propositions *as distinct from* both sentences and statements, and Aristotle scarcely makes these distinctions.

statements, but by exploiting the implications of the modal principle responsible for the trouble. If 'always true' entails 'necessarily true', then 'sometimes true and sometimes false' is equivalent to 'neither necessarily true nor necessarily false', i.e. to 'contingent'. This permits Aristotle a characteristic solution to his problem: the statement about tomorrow's battle is in a way contingent though in a way not. For the only genuinely contingent statements on this view are those whose truth-value changes, i.e. ones of the form: 'There is a battle'. The corresponding dated statements stand to these as instances to a type. So whoever links battling to a definite date makes a statement which although in a way necessary or impossible is an instance of something contingent. We can call it 'contingent', meaning by this that other instances of the same type have a different truth-value (the type thus being sometimes true and sometimes false). It is only to this extent that Aristotle succeeds in defending the contingency of tomorrow's battle.[15]

To support this interpretation Hintikka relies heavily on 19a23 ff.:

What is necessarily is, when it is; and what is not necessarily is not, when it is not. But not everything that is necessarily is; and not everything that is not necessarily is not. For to say that everything that is is of necessity, when it is, is not the same as saying unconditionally [ἁπλῶς] that it is of necessity. (Hintikka's translation, p. 156.)

As he understands it, 'when it is' functions as a schematic date, and the contrast with 'unconditionally' ('ἁπλῶς') is between an event described as occurring at a specified time and the same (type of) event described without definite temporal reference. On this construal Aristotle says in the third sentence that although dated statements are necessary or impossible the corresponding undated ones may not be, so that contingency is not ruled out.[16] In that case the first sentence must mean: 'If $p/\sim p$ at t_n, then necessarily $p/\sim p$ at t_n'; but it requires imagination to find this in Aristotle's actual words. There are more natural interpretations of the passage,[17] but Hintikka does not stop to refute them.

---

[15] See Hintikka, Ch. VIII, sections 3–10.   [16] Hintikka, p. 158.

[17] See above, pp. 89 f. For close criticism of Hintikka's, see Sorabji, pp. 133–4.

At any rate he sums up the main argument of his chapter in these words:

I have suggested that Aristotle considers the occurrence of a sea fight tomorrow contingent because in similar circumstances in the past and in the future it sometimes is true and sometimes false to say 'a sea fight will take place tomorrow'. In other words, if one asserts the contingency of tomorrow's sea fight, one is not any more speaking of *this* naval engagement; one is speaking, however elliptically, of similar sea fights in the past and in the future. (p.172.)

That is, one is saying elliptically of the corresponding calendar-dated statements that some are true and some false. This echoes an earlier remark:

Statements of possibility were taken by Aristotle to be primarily statements of relative frequency, wherefore they involve a range of cases. Saying that an individual event is possible is for him normally an elliptical way of saying that the relative frequency of similar events on similar occasions is different from zero. (p.162.)

When it comes to applying this to the text of *De Interpretatione* Hintikka's confidence wavers (see p.172, beginning of the penultimate paragraph), because on an unprejudiced reading of the chapter it is hard to believe that Aristotle is not concerned above all to uphold the genuine contingency of particular future events in all their particularity. He is defending (and in his own opinion successfully) the point of view of the agent: one who sees himself as originating this rather than that particular state of affairs, when both were real possibilities. If Hintikka's main view is right, and the contingency of the outcome consists only in the fact that in this particular case it was always necessarily true/false, but in others necessarily false/true that some such event should occur, then either the agent is powerless to make a difference, or he functions only as an intermediate link in a chain of causes fixed from eternity.

Accordingly, Hintikka appends to his main discussion a sketch for an ingenious alternative solution meant to preserve his central idea (viz. that contingent statements are sometimes true and sometimes false) while allowing for the contingency of particulars. He suggests that even when 'There will be a sea-battle tomorrow' refers to one particular date, Aristotle regards it as capable of change in truth-value from moment to moment between now and then. If at t_n today the facts are such as would naturally lead to a battle tomorrow, then at t_n the statement is true; if at a later time t_o today they change so that a battle tomorrow is no longer likely, then at t_o it is false. The battle itself is contingent if and only if there is such variation (pp. 172-4).

This account depends on a view of truth according to which the statement may be true even though the battle does not take place. There is no clear evidence that Aristotle ever entertained this idea,[18] and in any case *De Interpretatione* 9 provides one definite indication that here it is nowhere near his thoughts. For at 18b17ff. he argues that 'There will be a sea-battle tomorrow'/'There will not be a sea-battle tomorrow' (the reference is to the same day) cannot both be false. But on Hintikka's suggestion they very well might be, one after the other. And even so it is not clear how this preserves contingency in any sense that can satisfy the presuppositions of agency. If it is true at t_n, then false at t_o, that E will occur at some later date t_p, then presumably it was always, hence necessarily, true that 'E will occur at t_p' would be true at t_n and false at t_o. But in that case the corresponding variation in the facts must always have been necessary, and owes nothing to an originating agent acting so as to bring about E or prevent it.

Thus the general conception of contingency which Hintikka ascribes to Aristotle fails to stave off the determinism envisaged in *De Interpretatione* 9. Hintikka himself admits this, but is not on that account disposed to alter his interpretation.[19] His claim is not that Aristotle's solution is satisfactory, but only that it is the best available, given the assumptions about truth, omnitemporality and necessity with which (in Hintikka's view) he operates.

But if Hintikka is right about these assumptions, not only is Aristotle's solution inadequate, but the form of his problem is incomprehensible. For him, the defence of contingency is the defence of a contingent *future*: with past and present events the question cannot arise. It is this modal

---

[18] Hintikka himself cites as counterevidence *De Gen. et Corr.* I.11, 337b4 ff.: 'If it is true to say that X will be, it must later be true that X is'.

[19] Cf. Hintikka, pp. 161, 175.

asymmetry that Hintikka's account totally fails to explain. In the crucial passage already quoted Hintikka says:

I have suggested that Aristotle considers the occurrence of a sea fight tomorrow contingent because in similar circumstances in the past and in the future it is sometimes true and sometimes false to say 'A sea fight will take place tomorrow'. (p.172.)

However, sometimes it is true, and sometimes in similar circumstances false, to say 'A sea-fight took place yesterday'. Why does this not count as contingent too, if variation in truth-value is what contingency is?

To bring his account into conformity with Aristotle's modal asymmetry Hintikka must rule that the use of the past tense excludes application of 'contingent'. But the rule is simply added *ab extra*; it has no basis within the concept 'sometimes true, sometimes false'. And once it is adopted, the alleged connection between 'always' and 'necessarily' becomes suspect. Take 'A battle occurred at t_{-n}' and 'A battle will occur at t_{+n}'. The first if true will be so always. Is this the reason for calling it necessary? If so, the asymmetry rule is not being put to use. If on the other hand the former owes its necessity to the past tense, it follows that truth for an infinity of time is not the only source of necessity. Are there then two kinds of necessity both of which belong to the past-tensed statement, whereas its future-tensed counterpart has only one? But if one kind is not based on 'always' (or 'for an infinity of time'), why should we suppose that 'always' is the other kind's sole ground? If Hintikka takes due account of the Aristotelian temporal asymmetry of modality, his own approach ceases to be homogeneous and so loses much of its intellectual appeal. He might answer that since Aristotle's modal thinking is anyway based on a fundamental confusion,[20] it is no surprise that the results fail to add up to a systematic theory. The material was flawed from the start, so naturally the product does not hang together. Aristotle in fact neither has this excuse nor needs it. I have already argued against the charge of original confusion, showing that a number of his apparently

[20] See above, pp. 13 ff., 53 ff.

anomalous moves and positions can be explained without assuming him modally incoherent. The temporal asymmetry of necessity and contingency can likewise be explained on those terms, as the next few pages will show.

To return to Hintikka: as regards asymmetry his second suggestion is no more illuminating than his first. The second was that where 'There will be a sea-battle tomorrow' is taken as referring to one particular day, it is contingent if between now and then the situation changes so that at one moment it is such as to lead to a battle and at another moment not. But nothing is said to explain why this makes sense only if a future date is specified. Let us call the day 'Day Q' instead of calling it 'Tomorrow'. Suppose then that at t_n, prior to Q, there is a situation S of a sort that would probably lead to a battle on Q, and suppose also that at t_o, also prior to Q, S no longer obtains. It is always true that S prevails at t_n and not at t_o, and therefore always true that the state of things is different at those two times. If contingency depends simply on such variation, why is it not also *always* a contingent matter whether or not the battle occurs on day Q—even, for instance, when Q no longer lies in the future? And why should the contingency depend on variation in the state of things prior to the presumed date, rather than, say, immediately afterwards? The answer is evident: variation beforehand means that the causes of the battle's occurrence or non-occurrence are not yet settled: hence it is not yet determined and so still contingent. Certainly; but if contingency is analysed solely in terms of *variation* there is no way of making this point.

The modal asymmetry of the future rests on the unidirectionality of change: becoming is from earlier to later. In a vague way this connection is obvious, but its exact nature and bearing on the present topic require to be discussed in some detail. I shall argue that it is only in so far as change is regarded as *caused* that it is seen as unidirectional; and that changes in truth-values are not strictly speaking events at all, let alone caused events. From this it turns out to be no surprise that an account which locates Aristotle's modalities on the level of language fails to explain his modal asymmetry of past and future.

New situations are realized through change, and the change is a change *to* the situation realized. S is realized contingently at t_n if and only if a different time holds the possibility that S should be realized at t_n, and also the possibility that not-S should be. One of these two relative possibilities entails a change, since at t_n either S or its contradictory is a new situation by comparison with that obtaining at the time when both are possible. So a contingently realized situation is either itself the *terminus ad quem* of an actual change, or has an unrealized contradictory which is the *terminus ad quem* of a possible one. But change is necessarily from earlier to later. Therefore, since S is contingent only in relation to a state of affairs from which either it or its contradictory is a *terminus ad quem* of possible change, the state of affairs in question must have preceded the realization of S. So it is not any realization of S that is contingent relative to a given state of things, but only its realization in the future.

This spells out the dependence of the modal asymmetry of past and future on the unidirectionality of change. So far, nothing that we have said could not also have been said in terms of changing truth-values. For in so far as these change, the change reflects the direction of change in the world, so that what was true becomes false later than when it was true.

But why is change necessarily from earlier to later? We might say: 'There is a change from p to not-p' simply means 'p precedes not-p'. But if this is so, why is there no concept 'B- (= backwards-) change', i.e. one that stands to 'change' as 'succeeds' to 'precedes'? The answer must be: if 'There is a change from p to not-p' amounts to 'p precedes not-p', then there *is* such a concept, for it is identical with '— succeeds —'; only we do not happen to have another term for it in the way in which (according to the hypothesis) 'change from — to —' is an alternative term for '— precedes —'. On this view, the concept of change is built out of two components: one generic, invoking a *terminus a quo* and a *terminus ad quem*, while the other determines their earlier-later order. Unless the first component in some way intrinsically involves the second, there is no reason why we should not frame a parallel concept of B-change, in which the generic element reappears unaltered, while the other prescribes the opposite temporal order. Thus change and B-change would be conversely related species of the same genus, just as 'being the wife of' and 'being the husband of' are species of 'being married to'. The event described as a change from p to not-p may equally be described as a B-change from not-p to p. And while it is necessarily true, because analytic, that change is from earlier to later, it is just as necessarily true that B-change is from later to earlier.

If this is the situation, then it follows that the modal asymmetry between future and past, in so far as it depends on the unidirectionality of change, depends on a fact of language comparable to the fact of language whereby '— is wife of —' "runs" from female to male, not vice versa. It is simply true by definition of 'change' that there is no change to earlier, and so (by the connection of change with contingency) that only later events are contingent. But if it is coherent to suppose B-change, then why not also B-contingency? After all, if the contingency of a later situation, p at t_n, is shown by the fact that an earlier situation is consistent both with p/t_n and with $\sim p/t_n$, then the B-contingency of an earlier situation may be spelt out in the corresponding way. And if we say: but the earlier situations are in no sense contingent unless there is a possible *passage* from the present state of things to one or the other, the answer is that the passage, if there were one, would be a B-passage, the idea of which has not been shown to be incoherent.

But the apparent lack of a concept 'B-change' is also real, or at least not due to a shortage of vocabulary like that of a community whose family institutions resemble ours but who lack the phrase 'is wife of' while possessing the correlative. This point, however, will become clear only when we consider change in relation to causality.

Change, for Aristotle, is always caused change. In this context, what concerns us is the efficient cause.[21] A cause causes some object to be somehow different from how it would have been but for the cause. If what is caused is a change

---

[21] Cf. e.g. *Physics* III.3, 202b26–9, where κίνησις is defined as the actuality of a potential agent *qua* potential; ibid. VII.1, 241b24 ff.; VIII.4 *passim*; *Categories* 4b10 ff. (on which see below, pp. 136 f.).

(which it need not be, since things may be caused to continue in some condition when otherwise they would have changed), then what is caused is a state S_2 different from and contrary to the state S_1 which previously obtained. Now the cause ot change does not cause the earlier state S_1. For to say that it causes a difference from S_1 is to imply that but for the cause the object would have continued (*ceteris paribus*) in S_1. If then we were to say that the cause of change causes the earlier S_1, we should be committed to the absurd consequence that a cause produces, under the same conditions, a state of things that would have obtained had the cause not operated. This consequence is absurd because it nullifies the causality of a cause: there can be no effect that is identical with what (in the self-same situation) would have been present without the cause.

Now if the change in an object from its being F to its being not-F is also a B-change from not-F to F, then the cause of change is also a cause of B-change. In its capacity of causing B-change, we may call it a B-cause. Necessarily, perhaps, *causation* does not go from later to earlier, but there is no reason to suppose that this necessity is not of the same type as that which dictates the temporal direction of change. Hence, if the necessary earlier-to-laterness of change does not rule out the coherence of B-change from later to earlier, it should not rule out the coherence of later-to-earlier B-causality. So since the same event, say X's changing from hot to not-hot, may also be described as a B-change from not-hot to hot, we may also say that whatever cools X also B-heats it. These opposed descriptions prima facie no more contradict each other than 'X is to the left of Y' contradicts 'Y is to the right of X'.

All is well as long as we consider the cause, which is also a B-cause, as actually present and effective. Then we have an actual caused transition which can be described in two ways. It is otherwise when we consider what would have been the case in the absence of the cause (which is also the B-cause). It must be assumed that the structure of B-causation is the same as that of causation, except for temporal direction. For B-causation was introduced as a companion to B-change, which is assumed to differ from change only as '—— succeeds

—' from '— precedes —'. Since the (earlier) *a quo* of change is not an effect of the cause of change, the (later) *a quo* of B-change is not the B-effect of the B-cause. And in both cases, the state of things which functions as the *a quo* must be of the same character as the state of things that would have obtained (instead of the actual *terminus ad quem*) had the cause/B-cause not operated. Suppose, then, that X changes from F to not-F. Then there is a time t_n up to which X was F and after which it was not-F. If there had been no cause of this change, then the object would not have changed, and would have been F up to and beyond t_n. But the cause is also a B-cause. So if there had been no cause, there would have been no B-cause, and so no B-change. In that case, the state which is the *a quo* of the actual B-change would have occupied the time actually occupied by the corresponding *ad quem*. Hence, in the absence of the cause/B-cause, X would have been, after t_n, in a state identical (except for time) with the *terminus a quo* of change; and it would have been, before t_n, in a state identical (but for time) with the *terminus a quo* of B-change. But the *a quo* of the actual change is F, and that of the actual B-change not-F; so that both before and after t_n the object would have been F and also not-F.

'Change' and 'B-change' cannot describe the same concrete event. The analogy with 'precedes'/'succeeds' is exploded. They are opposed not as a relation to its converse, but as contrary relations. A better analogy would be with spatial passage, any one occurrence of which, if described as 'from P_1 to P_2' cannot also be described as 'from P_2 to P_1'. What our argument shows is that the same state cannot function as *ad quem* and *a quo* of one and the same concrete transition. It is obvious without argument that the same state cannot be both *termini* of a single change, nor of a single B-change, regarded simply as such. And once we relate change (and therefore its proposed counterpart) to causality, and then consider the counterfactual situation of the cause's absence, it becomes equally clear that the same state cannot double as *a quo* of a change and *ad quem* of a B-change regarded as one and the same event.

A limited modal asymmetry of future with past can now

be proved. If X is sitting at t_n, then his subsequent sitting at t_o is contingent at t_n only if a change is possible from sitting to some contrary. Suppose that such a change occurs. If it makes sense to say that from the standpoint of t_o his sitting at t_n is B-contingent, then it makes sense to say it in the possible case where there has in fact been a change. So, given that he is not-sitting at t_o, is his previous sitting now B-contingent? Only if a B-change is possible from not-sitting to sitting. Suppose the B-change to occur. Then it must coincide with the already-supposed change from sitting to not-sitting. So the earlier sitting is both *ad quem* and *a quo* with respect to the same transition, and the later not-sitting likewise functions twice over; which has been shown to be absurd. Therefore in any single case of transition, if one side is contingent/B-contingent from the standpoint of the other, the latter is not B-contingent/contingent from the standpoint of the first, and there is modal asymmetry.[22]

But this does not tie contingency as such to the future. Different transitions occurring at different times may, for all we have shown, have opposed directions. Unless this is impossible, the following situation is possible: X is sitting at t_n, and at t_n his sitting at t_{n+1} is contingent and his sitting at t_{n-1} is B-contingent. This description entails the possibility of a change to not-sitting and of a non-coincident B-change, also to not-sitting. In both, the sitting at t_n would function as *terminus a quo*. But nothing in what has been said implies that it would also be the *ad quem* of either transition. Hence the argument given above does not touch this case. However, suppose that the change and the B-change both occur, so that there is not-sitting at t_{n-1}, sitting at t_n, not-sitting at t_{n+1}. The sitting is preceded and succeeded by its contradictory, and X's state *varies* as between t_{n-1} and t_n, and as between t_n and t_{n+1}. Yet the sitting cannot be said to have come about through change in either direction. It is the *a quo* of both, but not the *ad quem* of either. It has neither become nor B-become, but simply *is*. Yet although the sitting is necessarily dissociated from becoming in either direction,

[22] In J.L. Mackie's terminology (*The Cement of the Universe*, Oxford 1974, pp. 178 ff.) the *a quo* is "fixed" and the *ad quem* "not fixed", although Mackie applies these terms to causes and effects respectively, not to the *termini* of change.

this is not because the sitting is everlasting or eternal. In short, we have a state which is new (looked at from either side) yet not the result of change. Indeed it is not clear that the sitting can be regarded as a result of anything, or as the effect of any cause. If a cause either changes an object or keeps it the same when it would otherwise have changed, and if the corresponding statement is true of a B-cause, then nothing is caused or B-caused unless either it or its contradictory is the *ad quem* of a change or a B-change. If the man had been not-sitting instead of sitting at t_n, then *ceteris paribus* this not-sitting would not have been the *ad quem* of either change or B-change, since on the hypothesis there would have been no variation at all. Given that he does sit, this state is still not an *ad quem*, for according to the construction of the situation it is an *a quo* in respect of both directions, and our previous argument showed that it cannot double as both *termini* at once. Hence it is not caused. Yet although not caused, it is necessary, and indeed doubly so, being neither contingent nor B-contingent; for either of these presumes it or its alternative to be a possible *ad quem*. All this suggests that if change is directional at all, i.e. if 'from — to —' has application, then it can have only one direction, by which I mean that there can be no opposite species of the same genus. (Thus the analogy with 'walking from P_1 to P_2'/'walking from P_2 to P_1' in turn breaks down.) Not only in any single event but in any single train of events it seems that to postulate more than one direction would force us into conceptual revisions extending far beyond any realignment indicated by the mere addition of one new term to the language.

Let us reinforce the conclusion with a final argument. Past events in general have effects outlasting them into the present. If the state of things at t_n is taken to include such an effect M, and if M is regarded as an effect of an earlier cause, but for which, *ceteris paribus*, M would not exist, then given the state of things at t_n, it is absurd to suppose the non-occurrence of M's cause at the earlier time. Hence from the standpoint of t_n, a past event regarded as cause of a present effect is not B-contingent. And in general, nothing is B-contingent from the standpoint of a time when its effects exist. So either no events are B-contingent, or some events have no subsequent effects. However, if the general conversion of directions were to make sense, it would make sense too to say that B-contingent events have B-effects that "outprecede" them into the more distant past. As before, this appears coherent until we try to combine it in one system with what is oppositely directed. Suppose that at t_n it is B-contingent that S obtained at t_{n-5}, and suppose that at t_{n-5} S did obtain. S has no subsequent effects, but presumably it was simultaneous with other events and circumstances whose non-B effects are now present at t_n. Let the B-contingent S be the burning of a bonfire of leaves, and suppose that a downpour occurred at the same time and place. Now did the rain affect S? Other bonfires (ordinary ones, with effects outlasting them into a later time) were extinguished, and the extinguishing too had its characteristic subsequent effects. But if the rain extinguished the B-contingent fire, either there were no effects (smouldering etc.) or they "outpreceded" that event "into" some yet earlier time. But now what do we mean by saying that the B-contingent fire was a bonfire of leaves at all? Do we mean that it was a fire that did not behave like a fire, since the attendant circumstances failed to make it react as normal fires react, viz. by giving way to a *subsequent* charred heap? Do we mean that it was not really a fire (since it did not exhibit behaviour definitive of the kind), but would have looked, felt and sounded like one, had we been present, so that we are entitled to say at least that it was *fire-like*? But even sensory appearances may depend on effects outlasting (in the direction of later) their cause, in which case nothing would have even appeared to creatures like ourselves, and to describe S we need words which for us could have no empirical meaning.[23] And if there was no appearance of S, would the human observer have seen something else occupying its supposed position in space? And even if S did appear to the human observer, it is not clear whether it can properly be said to have 'occupied a place' in an environment where it was not affected according to the

---

[23] For a more detailed argument to this conclusion, cf. S. Waterlow, 'Backwards Causation and Continuing', *Mind*, LXXXIII 1974, pp. 372–87.

known natural laws by normal neighbouring objects. It begins to be borne in that S can only be regarded as an element in a causal system if it consists in a B-fire which is B-extinguished by a B-downpour, B-warms B-animals in the B-neighbour-hood, all of which, in so far as they affect each other, co-exist only in a physical space not ours. In short, given that the direction of change and cause is from earlier to later, to suppose a world in which the contrary direction obtains is like supposing a dream-world. This does not explain why, in the world regarded as real by us, the one direction is from earlier to later. But it shows that the modal asymmetry of future with past can now be taken as established. For the genuine asymmetry of a relation in the real world is not contradicted by the possibility (if indeed it is possible) of our *dreaming* an internally coherent system in which the reverse relation holds; any more than the law of gravity has exceptions because a man dreamt that he was jumping over the Houses of Parliament.

If change is considered in isolation from causality, then there is probably no way of exhibiting the directionality of change: in other words, bracketed thus it has no direction apart from the temporal order of before and after, which may be taken either way, depending on whether we speak of it as precedence or succession. But since a cause of change stands in causal, not merely temporal, asymmetry to the *termini* of the transition, this is the most likely basis for the latter's direction, and so for the Aristotelian contrast between contingent future and necessary past.[24]

What a man thinks, says or writes may become false when it was true before, or the reverse: the direction of this becoming matches the direction of change in the world. But whereas so far we have spoken without demur of *change* in truth-values, for Aristotle this is not genuine change at all. It is not merely that it is derivative, in the way in which, for instance, the movements of an orchestra derive from and correspond to

---

[24] For Aristotle the directionality of change is further strengthened by the evaluative asymmetry between earlier and later presupposed by his teleology. However, this cannot be made the basis of a general argument, since even for Aristotle not all changes are governed by final causation.

those of the conductor; for unlike these, "change" of truth-value is not change except in at best a derivative and secondary *sense of the word*.

Aristotle is at pains to show this in *Categories* 5, 4a10–b19, where he discusses substances. He lays down:

It seems that the principal peculiarity of substance [*sc.* as opposed to entities in the other categories] is this: what is identical and one in number is receptive of contraries (τῶν ἐναντίων δεκτικόν) . . . For instance, numerically one and the same colour will not be white and black, and numerically one and the same activity will not be good and bad; and so on with the categories other than Substance. (4a10–17.)

With a different choice of examples the point might not be as obvious as Aristotle supposes: could not numerically the same activity be fast and (then) slow?[25] However, Aristotle's concern is with a different sort of counter-instance. For λόγοι and judgements (δόξαι) are, it seems, receptive of contraries, viz. truth and falsity, as the facts represented may change. And although he does not say how he individuates λόγοι and judgements, he clearly accepts that the change of truth-value applies to what is numerically one and the same in this sphere.[26] If, as is likely, he would individuate by reference to the time at which a particular subject had the thought or issued the utterance,[27] then he may be thinking of cases where my thought or statement becomes false even as I frame it. On the other hand, he might allow that a judgement or λόγος thus individuated can change in truth-value later, as suggested by remarks like: 'The judgement he made yesterday was true then but is now false'. This would imply that the identical judgement either somehow still has being (so as to remain as the subject of a new truth-value) even when its individuating circumstances are no longer present, or else changes value when it has itself ceased to be. Either alternative threatens the principle which Aristotle means to establish. For a particular that retains its identity when what individuates it is gone is certainly not a substance; and nor is a substance capable of receiving a contrary when itself no

[25] Cf. Ackrill, pp. 89 f.
[26] For a full discussion see Hintikka, Ch. IV.
[27] Cf. Ackrill, pp. 90 f.

longer exists. And even if Aristotle is only thinking of the
first type of case, i.e. where Callias gets up while the judgement 'Callias is sitting' is actually being framed, his problem
is essentially the same. For the judgement is formed of
elements which, he would say, are 'affections of the soul'
(i.e. of an ensouled rational substance) whose symbols are
linked in the external λόγος (*De Interpretatione* 1, 16a2 ff.).
Thus neither the judgement nor its verbal representation is a
substance, and yet in so far as they can change truth-value,
they are apparently 'receptive of contraries'. Nor would it
have helped him to have arrived at the concept of propositions
individuated independently of particular psychological and
linguistic events. For provided that the propositions are undated, and so can alter in truth-value, they challenge his
thesis, since whatever propositions are, they are not substances in the Aristotelian sense.

His reply, so far as it is effective, tells against all these
variations of counter-example, for his point is that change
in truth-value is not change. He declares first (4a28–b4) that
even if λόγοι and judgements can be said to receive contraries,
the essential distinction between substance and everything
else is that a substance receives its contraries through itself
changing ('αὐτὰ μεταβάλλοντα'), or through itself receiving
a change ('αὐτὸ μεταβολὴν δεχόμενον'). But:

λόγος and judgement themselves remain entirely unchanged [or: un-
changeable] in every way, although when the *thing* changes, the contrary [*sc.* truth-value] comes about with respect to them. (4a34–6.)

He then (4b4–18) argues that it is not even correct to say
that λόγος and judgement *receive* contraries.

For it is not because they themselves receive any contrary that they are
said to be receptive, but because the affection (πάθος) has occurred in
something else. For it is because the *thing* either is or is not that the
λόγος is said to be true or false, and not because it is itself receptive
of contraries. For strictly speaking neither λόγος nor judgement is in
any way changed by anything, so that they could not receive contraries, since nothing happens in them.

Here two further points emerge. Firstly he equates 'receiving
a contrary' with 'suffering an affection' and with 'something
happening in' the subject. Secondly, having already stated

that the λόγος does not change, he says that it is not changed in any way *by* anything, and on this grounds the conclusion that it is not receptive of contraries. For what receives, receives *from* something else, which is the agent *by* which it is affected, and what it receives is a πάθος in respect of which it is passive and the agent active. If, then, there is nothing *by* which the λόγος is changed, it receives nothing and suffers nothing.

It may seem that the force of this argument depends in the end on the non-substancehood of judgement and λόγος. For if change in the strict sense is defined as *suffering an affection*, it is hardly meaningful to ascribe this to any subject not a substance, if we take 'suffering' and 'affection' as charged with their ordinary associations. But why should change be defined in this way? Moreover, Aristotle would probably be hard put to it to give general criteria for what is to count as suffering an affection.[28] Ordinary usage would hardly sanction 'becoming healthy' as an instance, yet it is one of the examples which Aristotle gives here (4b14). But if we break with the familiar associations in this case, why not say also that becoming false and true are affections suffered by λόγοι? It is arguable that the only clear criterion for 'suffering' would turn out to be the logical one of *having a new predicate apply*, which covers changes alike in states of substance and in truth-values of λόγοι.

However, it is not only because λόγοι are not substances, and so cannot in the narrow sense suffer, that Aristotle refuses to say that becoming false or true is a genuine change. For, as he implies in the passages just quoted, the truth of a λόγος depends on its *relation* to a substance in the state predicated, and change in truth-value results when the *substance* alters so that the relation is different. On the side of the λόγος we register this by saying 'False now', but this phrase indicates only a difference of relation, not a change *in* its subject. From this point of view, the fact that λόγοι are not substances becomes irrelevant to the argument. For the distinction we feel between real changes *in* things, and merely

---

[28] In *Metaph.* Δ. 21 he only gives different types of case without attempting a unifying formula.

relational changes,[29] is best exemplified by cases where the subject of each is a substance. Phaedo grows and Socrates "becomes" shorter-than-Phaedo. In *Physics* V.2 Aristotle officially recognizes the difference with the brief remark:

> There is no change in respect of relation. For it can happen that when one of two correlates changes, a description becomes true of the other without its changing at all. Thus here the transition is accidental. (225b11–13.)

But 'accidental' is too vague to explain anything: here it does no more than relegate relational change to the edge of the topic of change proper.

The difference cannot be formulated in the logical vocabularies of the propositional and predicate calculi, even when supplemented with time variables or a 'T' operator.[30] But its rationale is forthcoming once change, as before, is treated as caused-change. Aristotle points towards this when, as in *Categories* 4b4ff., he connects change proper with agency and patiency. But our explanation does not depend on the archaic (whether or not obsolete) interpretation of efficient causality in terms of agent–patient. We may think of the cause as an event, if we like, and as a sufficient condition. All we need is the assumption (which even Hume accepts) that it is a condition of X's being the cause of a change that X should stand in some definite spatio-temporal relation to the latter.[31] If Phaedo grows, this is due to events and conditions in and around and contemporaneous with Phaedo, and to others more remote but continuous with these. But if Socrates without shrinking becomes shorter than Phaedo, this "effect" is not causally mediated by Socrates' circumstances in place and time. Wherever Socrates is, if Phaedo grows the new predicate applies. And wherever anything is that neither

---

[29] By 'merely relational changes' I am referring to cases where X comes to stand in a certain relation to Y for no other reason than that something has happened to Y which alters its relation to X. I do not claim that there are no "real" changes in respect of relational properties. Thus if Y marries, "real" change in his status must be described in relational terms; but if through Y's marriage X becomes the wife's great-uncle of Y, X has not on that account "really" changed.

[30] Cf. e.g. G.H. von Wright, *Norm and Action*, London 1963, pp. 27ff.

[31] "Action at a distance" is not ruled out, if the effect is assumed to vary with the distance.

grows nor shrinks, its size relative to Phaedo alters in step. Phaedo's growth and its causes, though natural events, would be of infinite power if these were their genuine effects. And their power would extend to the past and future and to the non-existent, since Phaedo probably grew taller than Rumpel-stiltskin, and Napoleon, and his own neolithic forebears. We have no less reason to say that they change than that Socrates does if our ground for ascribing change is that a new predicate applies. But that ground is absurd, given that change is caused: unless we are willing to view causation in any given instance as infinite or magical, unrestricted by time and space.

Change in truth-value is *par excellence* just such a pseudo-change. Judgements and statements may themselves be events caused by other events in consciousness or/and the nervous system. But even if so, and if also the very ideas with which we think are effects (mind- or brain-traces) of earlier causes, the intentional relation between thought and its object is not causal, nor does it extend between thinker and object along spatio-temporally continuous lines (as if, in order to think of the planet Mars we had first to summon up all that lies between). Thus a change in the object of thought does not as such produce a change in thought *qua* thought-of-that-object. But it is only in so far as thought is thought of-an-object that it is capable of truth, and of being at different times true and false.

If in abstraction from causality the distinction cannot be made between change and pseudo-change, this may explain why within the logical-empiricist tradition it has been something of a mystery to those who do not overlook it alto-gether.[32] The classical empiricist defining change as the succession of perceptions turns from this to causation as a separate subject. Yet he has the advantage over his more logically-conscious descendant, since he can dismiss Socrates' "becoming" shorter than Phaedo as unreal because it is no perceivable process. Whereas the latter's commitment to change as the succession of contradictorily describable states of affairs deprives him of even this resource.

[32] For recent discussions, see P.T. Geach, *God and the Soul*, London 1969, pp. 66, 71-2; T.P. Smith, *Ratio* 1973, pp. 325-33; P. Helm, ibid. 1977, pp. 34-8; S. Waterlow, *Nature, Change, and Agency*, Ch. IV, paras (14)-(17).

If change is unidirectional, and the Aristotelian modal asymmetry of past with future is a consequence of this; and if change is real and directional only *qua* caused; and if caused change is change in states of things in the world, not in truth-values of λόγοι: then Aristotelian modality belongs primarily on the level of things and their states, and is restricted by the general conditions governing the changes of these. If we look here for a further connection between 'always' and 'necessarily', 'possibly' and 'sometimes', we shall not be disappointed.

VII

The limits of the possible

What is possible is subject to certain universal restrictions, and also in each particular case to particular ones. It is the universal that will mainly concern us now. But before engaging in the final discussion, let me revert to a question raised but not answered in the previous chapter.[1] This has to do with the ontological status of the particular limiting factors. What is possible/impossible at a given time is restricted to what is possible etc. relative to the way things are at that time. The question was whether 'the way things are' is to be understood in terms of truth or extra-linguistic reality. We have so far spoken indifferently of 'that relative to which' as (a) a proposition (or set of propositions) true at a certain time, (b) a true proposition etc. dated with a certain date, and (c) an actual state of affairs obtaining at a time. However, if I have argued correctly that relative modality is not primarily a property of what is true or false, it follows that 'that relative to which' is also not primarily a λόγος or its truth. Thus it is relative to *the actual situation* at *t* in which X actually sits, that he has at *t* the possibility of coming to stand; and it is only because of a real relationship between the actual situation and his non-actual standing that it is also correct to say that the description of the facts at *t* is consistent with the *supposition* that he comes to stand. Again, if a man goes bald at *t*, then it is because of this actual state of things (which includes the laws of nature), that it is impossible at *t* that he should ever thereafter grow hair on his head; and it is the consequence (not the ground) of this that the corresponding propositions entail each other's negations. We must also say that it is because of the actual nature of space, as it is at any given time, that a commensurate diagonal is excluded for all time.[2] Finally, it is because a man actually sits at *t* that his standing at *t* is at *t* impossible.

[1] P. 117.   [2] Cf. Hintikka, p. 109 (footnote).

From this it follows that the present truth of a future-tensed statement in no way threatens its contingency. Earlier[3] it was pointed out that in assessing whether a supposition 'p' represents a state of affairs whose subsequent occurrence is possible relative to an earlier situation S, Aristotle has to assume that S does not include the prior truth of 'It will be the case that p' or of 'It will not be the case that p'. For otherwise no 'p' would be possible relative to S unless it was later true. From a purely logical point of view this exclusion may have looked like an *ad hoc* measure designed simply to avoid the consequence just mentioned. However, it then turned out[4] to accord with certain epistemic requirements for operating the suppositional method. But our latest discussion also shows the exclusion to be metaphysically justified. If the prior truth of a future-tensed statement were a genuine component of some actual earlier situation (in other words, if that truth were an earlier actuality), then indeed we should need a special argument (such as the epistemic one) to show that it is not arbitrary to leave it out of account when determining the RT-modal status of the corresponding event. But it now turns out that the truth as such has no call to be positively excluded, since it was never metaphysically in the running for inclusion in the actual situation relative-to-which. If the battle occurs, then it was earlier true that it would, and in some cases, perhaps, the occurrence was necessitated in advance. But where this is so the necessity is due to the character of earlier non-linguistic *actualities*, and the prior *truth* does nothing to enhance that necessity. Hence when the event is contingent, the prior truth that it would happen cannot diminish its contingency.

Some commentators on *De Interpretatione* 9[5] have thought that Aristotle's problem there arises from a conflict between the idea that the past is necessary, and the idea that future-tensed contingent statements already have truth-value. The conflict, it is said, stems from the fact that if 'p' is a statement true if and only if an event X occurs, then it is natural

---

[3] Pp. 50 f.
[4] Pp. 91 f.
[5] E.g. Cahn, pp. 38–9.

to say that the truth is due to the occurrence, and even that the occurrence *makes* '*p*' true. Now if truth-value is granted to future-tensed statements about contingent events, and if X is contingent, then if X does occur, it was earlier true that it would. Moreover if this much is allowed, there can be no reason to deny that what was true was *always* earlier true. But if the statement was true (even if unknowably so) before X happened, how can the happening *make* it true? If we say after all that the occurrence does not make it true, then we have to give some other account of the relation between what happens and the truth that it would. Since these two things are linked, if the latter does not depend on the former, the dependence must run the other way. That is: it must be because it was true that X would happen that X eventually happens. But then X cannot be regarded as ever having been contingent, since its occurrence is grounded in something which has held from all eternity. Thus to preserve contingency, we must say that the truth is due to the event, not vice versa. But how can this be, when before the event the statement was true already? The question has a double thrust owing to the ambiguity of 'already'. It may mean 'anyway', i.e. 'regardless of the event'. In that sense it is self-contradictory to say that the event makes true what was true *already*. On the other hand the word may simply mean that the statement was true *from earlier*. But on this interpretation the idea of 'making true what was already true' seems to fare no better. If it is not downright inconsistent, it still apparently harbours a conceptual absurdity, implying as it does that the event makes the statement to *have* been true. For to say this is to say that the event has (or should we say 'had'?) results that long preceded its own occurrence. But if the event really is contingent (until it occurs), then whatever results from it must (until then) be contingent too. Thus at all times before X occurs not only is it contingent whether it will, but also whether 'X will occur' has already been a truth from time immemorial. So up until the occurrence the past at each moment is not wholly settled and necessary. If we insist otherwise, we have to agree that the prior truth was always necessary and the corresponding event non-contingent. The only way, it seems, for Aristotle to escape this dilemma is to refuse to ascribe prior truth-value at all to the future-tensed statement.

Two chapters ago I argued that *De Interpretatione* 9 is not to be understood as an attack on the concept of prior contingent truth. At that stage it was not possible to consider the dilemma just proposed, since the reply depends on the modally significant difference between truth and actuality, and this had not been discussed. Now we are in a position to see through the paradox. The past is necessary because events and states of affairs cannot be caused from a later point in time. But change in a statement's truth-value is not real change, not being the effect of a cause. By the same token, the being-for-ever-true of a true dated statement is not a for-ever-enduring state of affairs. It is no more an instance of genuine stasis than its opposite of genuine change. This applies to the always-having-been-true of a true future-tensed statement. It always was; but it was never an actual state of affairs. Hence it is not the *effect* of any event. If then we wish, as we might, to say that the truth was *due to* an event which happened later, there is nothing absurd in this. There could only be a paradox if the dependence were causal; but truth does not belong to the world of cause and effect, which is the proper locus of Aristotelian relative modality.[6]

Let me turn back to the actuality relative-to-which. Having established that this can no more be a truth as such than a truth as such can be a real effect, we may consider its structure more closely. For the sake of simplicity I have so far spoken of it as a state of affairs or situation. Those whose ontology, like Aristotle's, includes only substances need not object. In passing from the level of λόγοι to the extra-linguistic level what we first encounter is, of course, the objective correlate of a statement or proposition, and this is not a substance, since a substance as such cannot make a λόγος true or false. But once off the propositional plane we need not stay with "states of affairs". Any temptation to stick to these probably springs from the habit of treating modality as essentially propositional: for although states of affairs are not

---

[6] Cf. A.N. Prior, *Past, Present and Future*, Oxford 1967, pp. 121 ff. on the 'Ockhamist solution'; and Sorabji, pp. 101–3.

propositions they have propositional "shape". However, we can coherently construe the modalities as relative, primarily, to substances. We may say not only as before that the possibility of X's coming to stand is relative to the actual situation which includes his sitting; but also, and perhaps preferably, that the possibility is relative to (or belongs to) X *qua* in that situation. As Aristotle says, he *has* the possibility. It is perhaps less natural to say that he *has* an impossibility, e.g. of presently standing. And if we substitute 'inability' this suggests that he could be cured. I shall say therefore that X, *qua* sitting, is *excluded from* currently standing and is *not excluded from* coming to stand.

The details of such an account present problems. For instance, while the bald man is alive, he may be said to be excluded from ever growing hair on the head. When he is dead, the actual state of affairs still excludes this, but the man is not, it seems, now excluded from it. If we take 'excluded from' as applicable to substances (*qua* situated one way or another), should we when X is dead say something like: all present substances are, and all future ones will be, excluded from co-existing with X-as-hair-grower? Or is 'is excluded from —' like 'is remembered', applicable to what no longer exists?

But if the general shape of the account is coherent, decisions on matters of this kind may be allowed to depend on considerations of simplicity and convenience; at any rate I shall not pursue them here. The main point is that relative possibility/impossibility may be construed as a real property of substances, the other member of the pair being the privation of this property. Their structure then turns out to be remarkably similar to that of Aristotelian efficient causation. For an Aristotelian efficient cause is not a sufficient or necessary condition propositionally expressed; still less is it a set of true propositions suitable to function as premisses in a prediction or as answers to requests for explanation. Rather, it is some particular substance which, *qua* possessed of certain qualities and standing in certain physical relations, is the agent of its effect. Indeed, if 'causality' is a modal notion, which it surely is, then Aristotle's familiar position on efficient causality already locates modality in substances.

Hence if his less well-known notions of RT-possibility and -impossibility seem to make most sense if these are construed as properites of substances, we should not be surprised. In fact, we can go further and say that causal necessitation, on Aristotelian terms, is not merely similar to but is a species of relative impossibility. We arrive at this interpretation by focussing on the patient rather than the agent as the locus of necessity. That is, we must think primarily of the patient as necessitated to realize the effect-state S, rather than of the agent as necessitating it. We can then say that the patient-substance, *qua* thus and so at *t*, is at *t* excluded from realizing not-S for some subsequent period (beginning perhaps at *t*). 'Thus and so' will refer to the causally relevant qualities and also to proximity,[7] in a suitable environment, to the particular substance we regard as agent.

A seated man who is excluded from currently standing, and not excluded from coming to stand, is in a certain relationship to what is and is not excluded. But this is not a relation in the logical sense in which 'Rab' entails '$(\exists x)(\exists y) Rxy$'. '— is excluded from standing' and the like must be treated as complex monadic predicates. Construing them thus we may say that as wholes they designate actual properties of actual things, without implying that the possible and impossible standings are real. Nor are we committed to the view that even though the standings are not real, there are other real things, namely possibilities and impossibilities, to which the sitting man is related. This follows only if Aristotle's sentence 'X has the possibility of coming to stand' is construed dyadically, on a par with 'X has the tickets for the show', where the tickets are real even if the show is cancelled. We are right to sense a certain concreteness implied by the present-tensed 'has', but wrong if we take it as indiscriminately spread. A concrete substance is the subject, and the possibility ascribed holds at a certain time (and also place, if a substance's characteristics can be said to be where it is). But there is no reason to concretize *what* is 'had'.

---

[7] 'Proximity' must be taken in a wide sense so as to cover the case where agent and patient are the identical substance.

This account of modality as an actual property of the actual raises a metaphysical problem which some may take as a reason for rejecting it in favour of propositional modality. We have to accept that mental states and activities involve actual (because instantiated by actual thinkers) relationships to what is not real. But how can there be such relationships, even if in the logical sense they are not relations, except where mind is involved? Yet it is not in so far as Callias is a thinking being that *qua* situated in Sparta he is excluded from being currently situated in Athens. Aristotle's conception of modality is at the opposite pole from the view that assigns it to propositions in virtue of their meaning, or what we mean by them. Yet something like meaning turns up on the extra-linguistic level, if modality is transferred here. For the alleged real modal properties are structured so as to involve an intrinsic reference to what is not or may not be real. And the problem of how it is metaphysically possible that what is real yet non-mental can, real-ly, be thus intentional, is not solved by classifying modality as a complex monadic property. This classification may avoid logical absurdity, but not metaphysical paradox. There may in the end be an equal paradox about the intentionality of the mental, but even if so, is it philosophically justifiable to extend the problem further than is absolutely necessary?[8]

The question raises fundamental general issues which cannot be treated *en passant*. But at the moment we are concerned with Aristotle, and of him it can be said that of all philosophers he is least likely to see intentionality as a stumbling block for a realist account of modality. This is because his entire approach to the concepts of change and becoming presupposes that all physical substances have actual properties incorporating a relationship to what is not, and may never be, real. Becoming is not for him reducible to being. To say that an object is becoming F is not to say

[8] If Russell is right, we may not know how far that is. See 'The Philosophy of Logical Atomism', loc. cit., p. 227: '. . . there is no reason to suppose that all the verbs I am talking of [*sc.* intentional verbs] are psychological. One should always remember Spinoza's infinite attributes of Deity. It is quite likely that there are in the world the analogues of his infinite attributes. . . I should not say that all the verbs that have the form exemplified by believing and willing are psychological. I can only say all I know are.'

that it actually is F, or that it actually will be so. For the prediction may turn out false if the object is interrupted in its progress towards being F, yet it will still be true to say that it *was* becoming F. And this means more than that although the prediction turned out false, we were justified in making it. To say that something becomes is not simply to predict or to say that we have a right to predict, but to describe an objective feature of the external situation: which feature necessarily makes reference to what may never come about. Intentionality in this sense is not only not the prerogative of the mental, but in so far as it attaches to change and becoming, it is excluded from mental, or at any rate cognitive, states and activities. For reasons which we cannot discuss here, Aristotle holds that *qua* thinking we do not change (any more than the λόγοι "become" true), even though thinking is an activity and may proceed in stages.[9] Change, for him, is primarily physical: and physical changes *par excellence* are actual events whose very nature consists in their being directed towards, or "meaning", the non-actual.[10]

Having discussed certain formal features of the particular actualities which in any given case set limits to what is possible, let us turn to more general limitations. What is in general possible is the same as what can in general come about through change. The omnitemporal necessities restricting change are for the most part discovered only by experience, as Aristotle well knows. But in a certain class of cases he is in a position to lay down *a priori* what must be the case for change to be possible. The type of change to which I refer is the generation of natural organic substances. Like reproduces its like, and (apart from the few and scientifically unintelligible cases of spontaneous generation) like cannot come into being except through reproduction by like. From Aristotle's point of view this is not mere dogma; nor is it supported only by induction from the phenomena. It can be shown to follow

---

[9] See *Metaph.* Θ. 6.
[10] This is the gist of the definition of κίνησις in *Physics* III.1.

from a metaphysical causal principle together with his organic concept of substance.

The causal principle in question is that an effect is in some way a continuation of its cause. Since Hume we have learnt to ridicule scholastic formulae such as 'The cause formally or eminently contains the effect'. But the actual procedure of science gives the lie to the Humean alternative, which is 'Any thing may produce any thing'.[11] By this Hume means that a proposition of the form '— causes —' is equally acceptable for all pairs of values confirmed by the same set of perceived conjunctions. Thus, for instance, if 'B' and 'C' are alternative descriptions of the same type of event, then if 'A causes B' and 'A causes C' are equally supported by the same perceived evidence, these two causal statements are equally acceptable regardless of the difference of description. If, on the other hand, a C may also be described as a 'B', and if by so describing it we can bring it under a generalization in which the connection with A is supported by a wider range of cases, then 'A causes B' is preferable to 'A causes C'. But if Hume were to allow that the preference is ever justified otherwise than by a greater range of support, then he would, in effect, be allowing that the conceptual content *alone* of one description can give it special suitability to appear in the context 'A causes —'. And to admit this would be to admit that there is some kind of conceptual and *a priori* affinity (even if not analytic "containment") between the terms of an acceptable causal generalization. And in that case it is no longer so clear that Adam could not have claimed causal knowledge on first opening his eyes.

Thus by Hume's standard, for instance, if 'A' and 'B' describe types of events in terms of their primary qualities, and 'C' is a description in terms of colour and taste, then if 'B' and 'C' have the same extension, 'A causes C' is as good a law (or as good an expression of one) as 'A causes B'. And we should be no worse off if we were unaware that C's are B's and knew only 'A causes C', despite the conceptual disparity of these terms. From this point of view, "emergences" are no more theoretically surprising than non-emergences, and indeed

---

[11] *Treatise* I, iv, xiii, p. 173 (Selby-Bigge), Oxford 1888.

the distinction vanishes. Theoretical efforts at conceptual gap-bridging are a waste of time except so far as they increase our powers of prediction. But in practice one of the aims of science (whether or not its principal aim) is to relate disparate observed conjuncts by means of theories in which the properties of one are displayed as reflecting those of the other, or as manifesting the same underlying characteristic. This is the motive behind the search for conservation laws, whether of matter, motion, mass, momentum or energy; and in the various historical formulations of these abstract concepts the hope of balancing causes with effects in terms of one or another of them has played a significant part. Whether the attempt has been to show causes and effects as composed of the same concrete constituents differently arranged, or as embodying the same quantum of some abstract quality differently distributed, the principle is the same.

The general requirement of causal continuity (which can receive any number of different empirical interpretations) sets a limit on what may be considered possible in a given physical system. What most concerns us here is the difference between systems in which the objects or events are regarded as products, in the logical sense, of their constituents, and systems where this is not the case. By 'logical product' here I mean a whole whose behaviour and properties are wholly determined by those of its constituents, while the behaviour and properties of these are determined independently.

In systems of the first type causal continuity does not exclude the possibility that there should come to exist complex objects of kinds never before instantiated. For if there exist the more elementary entities whose characteristics are such as to permit the unrealized combinations, these combinations could be[12] possible effects in the system, since the coming about of such a combination, should it occur, would consist only in the re-arrangement of what is already present, and the product would behave according to laws or combinations of laws already operative on a minuter level. Thus causal continuity would not be infringed by the coming to be of things

---

[12] I say 'could be' because the existence of the elements is only a necessary condition. We are speaking of relative possibility, which also requires that at some time their distribution is such that the combinations could result.

so far not exemplified in fact. But if no suitable elements were present, or elements of elements, then the non-existent complexes would be possible only in the sense that their descriptions are not self-contradictory; but not possible in relation to the actual world.

For Aristotle, the paradigm complex substances are not logical products of their components. They are organic structures of materials like flesh, bone, plant-tissue, etc. At a lower level, they are composed of his four basic inanimate elements, for it is into these that they eventually *de*compose. But the properties of the organic creature itself, and its behaviour, are not functions of those of the constituents. Metaphysically this follows from his conception of substantial unity. A white man is not as such a unity in the way in which a man is, although both are complex; and 'white man', unlike 'man', does not express a definable unitary concept.[13] For both 'man' and 'white' can appear in other complexes without alteration of meaning; and the white man not only shares his colour with other things, but his manhood makes the same contribution to the logical complex of which he is a "part" as it would make to the complex: dark-skinned man. Whereas the man himself, though physically complex, and the term 'man', though conceptually so (since otherwise it would be indefinable), are neither of them composed of elements which outside this context would behave in the same way and make the same contribution.

It is one thing to set up such a logico-metaphysical schema, another to claim that there are in the real world (which for Aristotle is the experienced world) entities possessed of this type of unity, which, he insists, is presupposed by all combination. And it is a third thing again to be in a position to claim to know which specific experienced objects are unities of this type. The fact that 'man' in 'white man' affords an illustration of the abstract point is no reason to suppose that an individual man is a genuine instance of what is illustrated. But considerations whose basis is at least in part empirical enable Aristotle to give content to the schema. His inanimate elements are simple masses without intrinsic structure, and

[13] *Metaph.* Z.4.

their natures are accordingly expressed in the simplest possible behaviour, namely rectilinear motion up and down. Thus earth falls, fire rises, etc. The view is clearly loaded with assumptions about simplicity and the metaphysical relation between an object and its behaviour; yet it is not without support too from ordinary observations. Now this motion of the elements is their only property, apart from their mutual transformability in a closed cycle. But these motions and transformations, however combined and compounded, could not begin to account for the structure, the formation, the stable continuance and the behaviour of organic creatures. Biological phenomena cannot be explained as the resultants of such simple forces as naive observation tends to suggest are all that is present in inanimate nature.[14] The organism of course depends on these, as for instance when in nutrition it assimilates external materials composed of the basic elements. But the consequent structured growth can only be explained by a different type of principle already present in the organism. Again, in reproduction, for the same reason, the parent or seed or fertilised ovum is not merely a place where minute portions of elements combine according to none but the laws of their own natures to form the starting point of a new member of the species. For the parent is required not merely as a "place" (nature's test-tube), but as a source of the organic principle. And this it can possess to transmit only if it is a creature of the same kind.

In short, in such a system an organic being such as had never before existed would be a pure "emergence". Thus to the extent[15] to which causal continuity prevails, to that extent the coming to be of a new complex kind is impossible, except in the non-Aristotelian sense that its description is not self-contradictory. In this way, we get a version of proposition A', linking possibility of existence to realization at some

[14] For a detailed discussion of the physics and metaphysics of Aristotle's holism in biology, see Waterlow, *Nature, Change and Agency*, Ch. II.

[15] The qualification is because of "spontaneous generation". Aristotle holds in effect that causal continuity does not apply to quite all organic kinds, as there are very low forms of life that arise from mud etc. (with which, being so low, they are *almost* continuous). He does not however hold that where it does apply, as in the case of highly organized species, it applies only to some or most members. In these cases (the vast majority) the causal principle holds without reservation.

time. Whatever can come to be (in Aristotle's narrower sense of 'come to be' where he means substantial generation) is (already) in some instance at some time realized.[16] More precisely: if at a given time (i.e. relatively to the state of things at the time) it is possible that a being of kind K should come to exist, then *at that time* there actually exists some being of kind K. It follows that if at a given time there are no K's, then at that time it is impossible that there should come to be K's ever after. And if at all times there are no K's, then at every time t it is impossible that there should ever come to be K's.[17]

Thus where K's are generated substances, we also get an existential version of proposition B' ('if always . . . then necessarily . . .'), namely: 'If it is always the case that there exist no K's, then it is (always) necessary that there should never be K's'. But this does not yet give us a positive version of B' linking omnitemporal with necessary being (as opposed to non-being). Such a positive version might take the form (B'1): If there always exist K's, then it is (always) necessary that there be K's; or else (B'2): If a K always exists, then it is (always) necessary that that K exist. The latter, with its reference to the same K throughout, more closely resembles the conclusion of *De Caelo* I.12, which was reached from dubious premises. Has Aristotle any better grounds for B'2?

This is best approached via B'1. However, neither B'1 nor B'2 follows from the requirement which establishes the above version of A'. Granted that an organism cannot come to be unless from an already actual member of the species, it does not follow that the species must always in future be instantiated, even given the fact that it always is. But the principle of causal continuity which excludes the emergence of species

[16] Cf. e.g. *Metaph.* Z.7, 1032a22–5 and Θ.8, 1049b24 ff. Hintikka takes note of this basis for A' (Hintikka, pp.105–7) but does not say how it can be reconciled with his view that Aristotle reduces modality to extensional terms.

[17] This and the preceding statement apply also to simple inanimate stuffs. The point needs to be made, since Aristotle holds that particular "parcels" of fire etc. are constantly coming into being and passing away; so why should there not come to be a mass of some entirely new simple stuff? Answer: no new mass of anything comparable to fire etc. can come to be otherwise than as a stage in an eternal *cycle* of stuff-to-stuff transformation; hence a type is instantiated only if re-instantiated (see *De Gen. et Corr.* II. 1–5; *De Caelo* III. 6).

can naturally be extended (an extension Aristotle takes for granted) so as to exclude their extinction. Thus as well as (1): 'Like comes from like', we have (2): 'In every generation like reproduces itself in sufficient instances to ensure the continuance of the species'.[18] The first postulate sets a limit to the possibilities for generation, while the second lays it down that the range of possibilities thus limited does not decrease. Between them they ensure that the contents of the universe at every stage of its history come under the same set of natural principles. For to Aristotle, a natural principle is what determines the characteristics typifying substances of a given species.

In a system such as his, the principle restricting the possible to what is prefigured in the actual does not entail that the range of possibilities will *remain* constant. That something was reproduced is not a logically sufficient condition for its reproducing in turn. If the organism fails to reproduce it will pass away into the inanimate elements of which it was composed. In this, the first postulate is observed since the elements are not emergences, having been in a sense present all along; but in themselves they can never come together to form another such organic creature. Thus there has to be a further principle to ensure that this entropic process is the exception not the norm, since otherwise the possibility for any creatures of the kind might eventually be lost.

From the two principles in conjunction it follows that if at any time t there exists a K, the species of K's is ingenerable and imperishable. For (a) it does not merely happen to be the case that there always have been K's, since there could not be any at t (for whatever t) if prior to t there had ever been none; and (b) it is never possible that K's should cease. Thus the instantiation of a species *even for a limited period* entails the necessity at all times that it be always instantiated.[19] *A fortiori* this necessity also follows from the premiss that the species is *always* instantiated. Thus we get B'1: 'If there

<hr />

[18] See e.g. *De An.* II.4, 415a24 ff.

[19] Cf. the way in which, by the *De Caelo* I.12 argument for B', X's being always-F at t (where t is some single selected moment) entails the impossibility at all times of its ever being not-F. See above, pp. 72 ff.

always exist K's, then it is always necessary that there exist K's'. B'1 and its relation to the proposition from which it has just been derived serve to illustrate the complexity of Aristotle's connections between time and modality. In the first place, the consequent of B'1 affirms the necessity that a certain sort of situation always hold. Secondly it affirms that this necessity obtains at all times. Yet this necessity, we now see, is not grounded in the 'always' in the antecedent of B'1; for the consequent of B'1 also follows from an antecedent in which 'for a limited period' or 'at t' takes the place of 'always'. There could be no clearer proof that Aristotle does not define 'necessary' as 'always'.

What now of B'2? This says that if some individual K always exists, then it is always necessary that it should exist. This follows from the two continuity postulates together with one more assumption to be mentioned presently. Suppose that there is an individual K which always exists. Then its nature as a K does not in itself tie it down to a limited natural span. However, perhaps it is vulnerable to destruction by external force. If this is possible for any individual of the kind, then it is possible for each, and there is no logical reason why it might not happen to all. In that case a time might come when no K's were left. But the continuity of nature demands that the species not die out. If the K's could cease, continuity would still be assured if it were certain that some of them would reproduce. Suppose then that this is so, but that all the same some K's do always exist as a matter of fact. It now seems that they do but need not, so far as the continuity of nature is concerned. However, the offspring must be of the same species. But the offspring by definition are generated. Hence some members of the species are generated and others not, since some have never not existed. But as members of the same species, it must be possible for the ungenerated K's to produce generated ones. For if generated K's could come only from antecedent generated K's, the causal powers of the generated and the ungenerated would differ so radically that they could not be said to be members of the same kind.[20]

[20] Cf. De An. II.4, 415a24 ff., where he says that reproduction is 'φυσικώτατον τῶν ἔργων' for the creatures capable of it. For 'φύσις' = 'essence' cf. Physics II.1, 193a30 ff.

Suppose then that the ungenerated produces the generated. But now it produces what in respect of being generated differs strikingly from itself. But since like is produced from like this is not possible. Hence the ungenerated cannot reproduce, and continuity therefore requires that it be of such a nature as to be indestructible.

This argument dispenses with the suspect *De Caelo* assumption that there is *an* infinite time, which is the maximal period for anything that lasts for ever. It relies instead on the principle of the continuity of nature, which is not so conceptually alarming. However, it further assumes that the property of being generated is not merely, as we have just said, striking, but also essential. For like need not come from what is like it in every respect. The characteristics essential to the species are the ones necessarily prefigured in the parent. Only if being generated were non-essential could a being that has always existed reproduce its kind in offspring. But from Aristotle's point of view nothing could be more unreasonable than to treat being generated as inessential. This is a point of view in which generation is bound up with development, and development is of the essence of creatures subject to it. Dominated as he is by a biological conception of substance, he would laugh at the suggestion that substances might come into being fully formed from the start.[21] Generation itself is only the first stage in a process not complete until the offspring is mature.[22] And in the developing creatures that we know, the stages and pattern of the process

---

[21] The idea of mature living creatures miraculously created *ex nihilo* is a legacy of our culture. If such a miracle is conceivable at all, then presumably it is conceivable as occurring even *within* the history of the natural universe. What is first thought of as possible from the extra- (or pre-) mundane standpoint of a divine creator may come to seem possible as an event with its own place in the actual temporal order (even if it is still assumed to be from a non-natural cause). But Aristotle, I have argued (cf. p. 48 above), has no means of framing the notion of 'possible from an extra-mundane standpoint'.

[22] However, Aristotle's account of the mutual transformations of the simple stuffs implies that particular "parcels" of these come to be all at once (in which respect their generation resembles certain qualitative changes: see, e.g., *Physics* VIII.3, 253b 25). But he is not always willing to rank the simple stuffs as substances proper: lacking structure, they lack the requisite unity (see *Metaph.* Z.15, 1040b5 ff.). He implies, in effect, that it is a mark of generated substance proper to be capable of development, since only a structured unit *can* develop.

are as much the stamp of the species as the mature characteristics. Being thus essential, the capacity for development is
necessarily transmitted to the offspring and by them necessarily received only through inheritance. Hence if an everlasting substance were to procreate, it too must be a product
of development. But development as we know it starts with
the first moment of life. So, since existence does not precede
development, the always existent, if it has developed, must
have been developing from eternity. Now if the continuity
of the species is to depend on the ungenerated's capacity for
reproduction, it must be possible for the ungenerated
actually to become mature enough to reproduce. This then is
a condition which at any given moment of time does not lie
infinitely far into the future. But the advance towards it
must at each moment of its occurrence have already been
occurring for ever. Has that process gone through various
stages? If not, it can scarcely be called 'development'. If so,
then the first stage at least can never have had a beginning.
In this alone its temporal structure is *toto caelo* different
from the putative offspring's first stage. Yet it was precisely
in order to assimilate the parent to its progeny that the
former was assumed to have been developing at all. But in
any case, can we even form the idea of a stage that had no
beginning? How can it be one among other stages of the same
process, any more than a geometrical point is one of the
fractions of a length? Our experience of organisms that are
born as well as die is the only foundation we possess for the
notion of 'development by stages', and in their case a mental
survey backwards cannot fail to reach a point before which
the creature did not exist even in embryo. Seen in these
terms, the only clear ones available to us, development can
no more be thought to lack a beginning in time than concentric waves a spatial point of origin. Hence we cannot trust
as coherent the notion of an everlasting individual substance
unless there is a built-in assumption that the individual is at
all times complete. And this absence of development cannot
be regarded as accidental. To say that the thing might have
happened to develop even though it did not is as much as
to say that it might have happened to be a substance of a
different kind.

A thing which always exists, then, not only never was generated, but is of a nature to exclude the very possibility that a being of its kind should ever come to be.[23] To suppose such a nature transmissible by reproduction is logically even more absurd than to suppose it capable of one day ceasing to be exemplified at all. If, however, the principle of natural continuity is assumed necessarily to prevail, then for an individual that always exists its endless existence must be deemed no less necessary. For there can be no future generations to which to hand over the task of sustaining *in perpetuum* the instantiation of the species.

[23] For a similar position concerning perishing, see *Metaph.* I.10.

VIII

Conclusion

That Aristotle merges modal with extensional concepts is a baseless charge, appearances notwithstanding. The "appearances" are his doctrines A′ and B′ which link possibility and necessity with realization at some and at all times. Correctly interpreted these propositions support the opposite view, that for him these connections are syntheses of irreducibly different concepts. If the interpretation is not obvious, it is because A′ and B′ incorporate a multiplicity of more or less obscure references to time. These are liable to confusion not only because of the temporal theme in common, but because the concepts and principles in play here lie off the main tracks of modern analysis. By Aristotle on the other hand they are so far taken for granted that he lacks the motive to labour explanations.

In the first place there is his temporalized approach to modality, whereby possibility is seen as relative to an actual state of affairs in the history of the universe. Time has a double bearing here, since the possibility itself belongs at a time, as would the realization should it occur. This is Aristotle's central and, I have argued, his only conception of possibility; but although coherent enough in itself it has in recent times attracted only a minute fraction of the formal attention given to the absolute modalities, and when noticed at all has usually been defined in terms of these.[1] Secondly, A′ and B′ in the versions considered here depend on non-formal assumptions cogent only in the archaic context of Aristotle's organic metaphysic of substance. Time enters in here too as a dimension in which states and activities may be

---

[1] See e.g. H. Reichenbach, *Elements of Symbolic Logic*, New York 1947, pp. 384 ff.; W. Sellars, 'Fatalism and Determinism' in *Freedom and Determinism*, ed. K. Lehrer, New York 1966, pp. 163 ff.; Rescher and Urquhart, *Temporal Logic*, New York 1971, pp. 206-7. An exception is S. McCall, op cit., pp. 426 ff., esp. pp. 435-6.

realized to a point of completeness whose attainment sets an unimposed bound to the duration of the condition.

A′ and B′ require both this logic and this metaphysics, each of which could occur without the other. Theoretically, Aristotle could have spelt out modality in absolute terms while retaining his fundamental notion of substance as organic unity. He could not then have reached A′ or B′ unless by a fallacy. On the other hand, the temporalized notion of possibility may also be used in conjunction with a non-organic metaphysics, and in this context too there would be no foundation for A′ and B′.

These doctrines in their various Aristotelian forms carry no threat of total determinism. Nor do they entail that in general something is possible only if something similar is actual. The metaphysical components in the different versions, those of *De Caelo* and those discussed in the previous chapter, apply only to a limited range of possibilities. For non-logical reasons these have to be actualized, but there are others that need not ever be in any instance, without prejudice to their conformity with Aristotle's RT rule for 'possible'. Thus so far as A′ and B′ are concerned there exists a genuine field for chance and for voluntary agency. If I am right, the only danger to this that he envisages lies in a rigid insistence that all assertions are erroneous if untrue.

So A′ and B′ entail no general coincidence of the actual with the possible, for either particulars or types. And even in the range of cases for which these propositions hold, the logical situation is not as Professor Hintikka takes it to be. He claims that Aristotle is in effect committed to viewing the difference between necessity and contingency as nothing more than "statistical" or quantificational, the difference between 'all' and 'some but not all': a view which Hintikka is surely right in arguing that Aristotle could not have endorsed except through gross confusion. But at any rate in *De Caelo* I.11–12 Aristotle shows that he himself would be amongst the first to declare against any such position. In its own long-obsolete terms the proof articulates a clear perception of the fundamental difference between necessary and contingent being. For the connection between the temporal quantifiers and the modal operators is mediated by a nonquantitative reference to time. The linking propositions are of the form: 'X is always-F/always-not-F' and 'Y is for-a-finite-period-F and (at some other time) for-a-finite-period-not-F'. The temporal terms here are integral parts of the predicates, or as Aristotle puts it, the subject's F-ness is in each case the realization of a capacity defined by reference to the temporally maximal exercise. Hence things that are always F and things that are F and then not F are at no time engaged in some common activity in the one case inter-mittent and continuous in the other. The heavens are always in motion,[2] while terrestrial substances move and cease moving; but these motions are not longer and shorter versions of the same general kind of thing: no more than an epic and a sonnet that both treat of the same theme.

I have mostly been concerned to urge the difference be-tween the formal modal elements in A' and B' and those imported by the metaphysics of organic substance; but on a highly abstract level certain common features may be dis-cerned. Both sides relate to the world of concrete substances where change happens and causes operate. Aristotle's modali-ties are rooted here, not among concepts or propositions or the linguistic expressions of these, although he happily allows them a derivative purchase on this level. Unless this is recog-nized, the modal asymmetry of past and future, traditionally accepted as integral to Aristotle's approach to modality, ought rather to be treated as a mere addition. For the asym-metry follows the direction of caused change, whereas shifts of truth-value are not events in any causal nexus.

Finally, A' and B' represent his double rejection of that combinatorial approach whose ancient pedigree and massive success in later logic and science have inclined some philo-sophers to accept it as a virtual dictate of the natural light. As logician he does not consider analysing necessity in terms of tautological or inconsistent combinations of simple pro-positions or sentences. As metaphysician and scientist he repudiates attempts to explain complex but unitary physical

---

[2] The example is not ideal, since motion and its kinds are not modes of categorizable *being* (see above, pp. 61 ff.), but rotation is virtually the only empirical attribution of Aristotle's 'things that always are'.

phenomena as products of existentially independent components. In any correct account, "that for the sake of which" must figure as controlling the behaviour of wholes and hence the contribution of parts. Any attempt to represent this as another component among components will only trigger the search for a further end for the sake of which all *these* are co-ordinated together. Just so, no proposition or set of propositions is necessary, contingent or impossible unless something is actual, and although this too may be described by a proposition, its *actuality* finds no place in any propositional set.

Index

Can you tell a gull from a tern? A toad from a frog?
A Petoskey stone from honeycomb coral?
Do you know why some sand is black?
Which bird on this page is a sandpiper?

Find here easy clues to more than a hundred natural
Great Lakes wonders on U.S. and Canadian shores.
Learn to recognize loons and cormorants,
stones and fossils, toads and turtles, butterflies
and dragonflies. Start treasure hunting now
on your favorite beach, or right in these pages.

ISBN 0-9708575-2-7

$ 12

9 780970 857521

Beaver island A

989-894-5925
BeaverIslandArts.com

Mary Blocksma has authored eighteen children's books and four
books celebrating the Great Lakes. Her work has been featured
by the Junior Literary Guild, Reading Rainbow, the Rodale
Book Club, Quality Paperback Book Club, *Scientific American*,
and countless school and library reading lists. Other books
by Mary Blocksma include *What's In the Woods? A Great Lakes
Area Treasure Hunt*, *Great Lakes Nature*, *Lake Lover's Year*,
and *Necessary Numbers*.

WHAT'S ON THE BEACH?

A Great Lakes Area Treasure Hunt

Art and Text by Mary Blocksma

Beaver island Arts

What's On the Beach?
A Great Lakes Treasure Hunt
First Edition, Second Printing
Copyright © 2003, 2012 by Mary Blocksma

For information on obtaining permission for
reprints and excerpts, or obtaining prints,
notecards, original art, or educational support material, please contact the publisher:

Beaver Island Arts
P.O. Box 40
Bay City, MI 48707-0040
989-894-5925
BeaverIslandArts.com

Printed in the United States of America
    10 9 8 7 6 5 4 3 2

Cover art, design, and photo by Mary Blocksma

Cataloging-in-Publication Data:

Blocksma, Mary.
        What's on the beach? : a Great Lakes treasure hunt /
art and text by Mary Blocksma.
        p. cm.
        Includes index.
        SUMMARY : Introduction to natural wonders along the
Great Lakes shoreline shows readers the difference between
a gull and a tern, why some sand is black, how to tell if bears
have been nearby, and much more.
        Audience: Ages 6-12.
        ISBN 0-9708575-2-7

1. Zoology--Nomenclature (Popular)--Juvenile literature.
2. Plant names, Popular--Juvenile literature. 3. Natural
history--Great Lakes Region--Juvenile literature. [1. Animals.
2. Vocabulary. 3. Plant names, popular. 4. Natural history.]
I. Title.

QL355.B56 2003   508.77
                                        QB133-1251

To Marie Marfia and M. Martin Sielinski
without whom I could not have done this book

Acknowledgements

My endless gratitude belongs to Marie Marfia of Dancing Mac Graphics, Ludington, Michigan, and artist M. Martin Sielinski of Bay City, Michigan, for generous expertise, countless rescues, and warm friendship. I also thank Earl Wolf, Education Outreach Director, Michigan Department of Natural Resources, and Dennis A. Albert, Ecology Program Leader, Michigan Natural Features Inventory, Michigan State University, for their many helpful suggestions; Nancy Garard, special education teacher in Saginaw, Michigan, for her knowledge of elementary and special education curriculums; Sue Blondin, elementary school teacher in Bay City, Michigan, for excellent proofreading; Thomas Starkweather of Bay City for helpful suggestions; and Richard Clayton of the *Bay City Times* for welcome Quark solutions.

More thanks go to my long-time friend and colleague Marylee MacDonald, editor of the *River Oak Review,* Evanston, Illinois, for editing savvy; and to William A. Lewis, art professor *emeritus* of the University of Michigan, and artist Garland Lewis, for their encouragement and feedback. Special acknowledgement is made to Richard A. Paselk, Chair of the Chemistry Department, Humboldt State University, for his fossil photograph; and to Mary Rose Scholl of the Beaver Island Toy Museum and Store for the loan of a fossil. Very special thanks belong to Larry L. Smith and my son, Dylan K. Kuhn, for always believing. Any errors in this book are mine. M.B.

Contents

Author's Note

   This is a beach book for amateur naturalists of any age. Find here easy clues to naming more than a hundred Great Lakes wonders, plus two beaches to practice on. Take this book to the beach or do your treasure-hunting right in these pages.

   It wasn't easy to choose from the huge variety of summertime plants, stones, fossils, insects, birds, and other animals that appear on or near our many Great Lakes shores. I looked for those which were easy to identify, although many can also be found in other habitats. And, of course, everything will not appear on one beach. You may have to explore several kinds of beaches if you want to find all of these treasures.

   I believe that we take better care of things we can name. I offer this book as a playful beginning. Look for more information on my website. Please visit me at http://www.beaverislandarts.com.

                                                            —Mary Blocksma

Which Great Lake?

Where do you go to the beach? Find the Great Lake closest to your home. Then choose a spot on this map near your favorite beach or a beach you would like to visit.

Which beach?

Does your beach look like any of these? The more than 10,000 miles of Great Lakes shores offer a happy dazzle of beaches. Most of them are rich in treasures you may not have noticed. Even if you've seen them, you may not have known what they were.

Can you tell a gull from a tern? a heron from a crane? chain coral from honeycomb coral? Do you know what the sand is made of?

Read on to find easy clues to these and many more Great Lakes wonders. Then go treasure hunting on your favorite beach, or on the beaches on pages 42 through 45.

Busy

Rocky

Quiet

Stony

Marshy

Grassy

Sandy

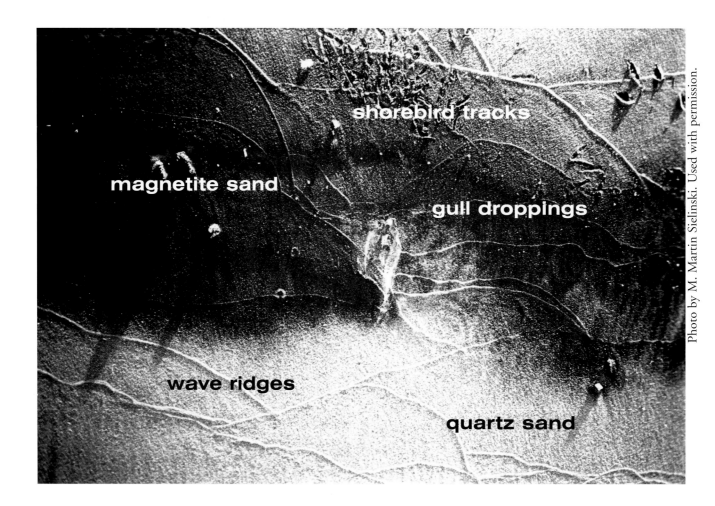

shorebird tracks

magnetite sand

gull droppings

wave ridges

quartz sand

What is sand made of?

Nine out of ten grains of beach sand are made of quartz (page 24). Sand grains up close often look like little cubes of glass. Black sand grains, however, are magnetite, not oil, dirt, or pollution. Magnetite grains are smaller than grains of quartz sand, but twice as heavy. Try collecting black sand with a magnet!

The wind is a sand artist. It sorts the sand into patterns by blowing the small grains farther than the large ones. The wind also moves the water which in turn moves the sand. Have you ever noticed how pebbles on a beach are often sorted by size? Sand is sorted much the same way.

Damp sand that squeaks when you scuff it is called singing sand.

Gull...

Do all gull-like birds look alike to you? Some are gulls, but others may be terns. There are many kinds of gulls and terns. These are just a few of them.

...or tern?

black head and body

Black Tern

A BROWN GULL is usually a young or adolescent gull!

Bonaparte's Gull

black head

black cap

Gull

Tern

black legs

Caspian Tern

black ring around bill

yellow legs

Ring-Billed Gull

A gull-like bird with a black cap or a black body is not a gull at all. It's a tern. Almost all terns have forked tails and graceful, pointed wings that flap in a regular way when they fly. Terns catch their own fish—and with pizzazz! Watch them hover high over the water, then plunge straight in!

Gulls are often bigger than terns. Gulls like to soar, circling on warm air currents called thermals. They don't fish very well, so they often try to steal their meals from terns and diving ducks.

Herring Gull

black cap

Common Tern

pink legs

orange legs

Diving duck...

Diving ducks eat fish. They can swim under water and sometimes disappear, popping up somewhere close by. Often diving ducks dine just offshore in large groups as they migrate north or south. You probably need binoculars to tell one kind of diving duck from another.

Puddle ducks eat plants. They often turn upside down—heads under the water and tails above—while they search for plant food. The mallard is one of the most common puddle ducks.

...or puddle duck?

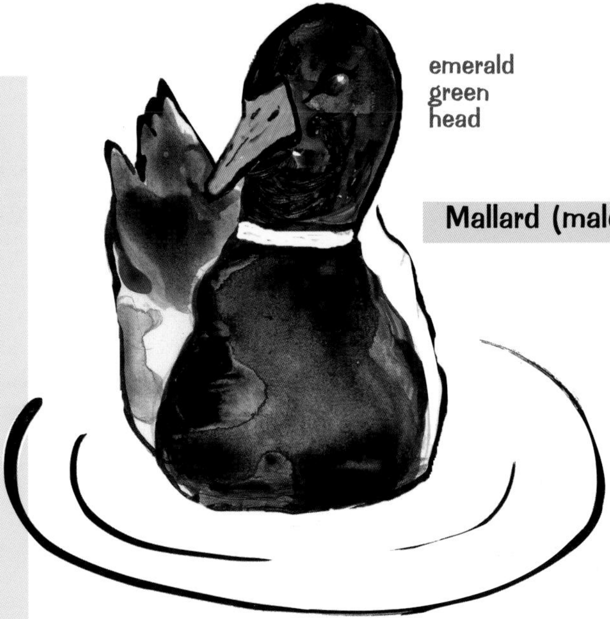

emerald green head

Mallard (male)

smooth black head

Common Merganser (Male)

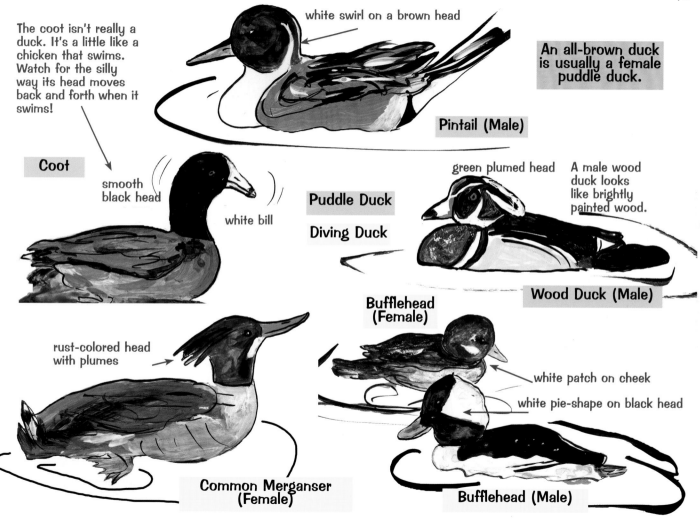

The coot isn't really a duck. It's a little like a chicken that swims. Watch for the silly way its head moves back and forth when it swims!

white swirl on a brown head

An all-brown duck is usually a female puddle duck.

Pintail (Male)

Coot

smooth black head

white bill

Puddle Duck

Diving Duck

green plumed head

A male wood duck looks like brightly painted wood.

Wood Duck (Male)

rust-colored head with plumes

Bufflehead (Female)

white patch on cheek

white pie-shape on black head

Common Merganser (Female)

Bufflehead (Male)

Canada Goose

white cheek patch

Geese and cormorants
often fly in V's.

Loon chicks ride on mom's back.

black and white body

Goose, loon...

Although the Canada goose feeds
on grains and plants, the loon and
cormorant eat fish. Their extra-heavy
bones let them swim deep under
water. Watch for big dark birds that
float oddly low in the water, like over-
loaded boats.

Canada geese and double-crested
cormorants often hang out in crowds.
Look for loons alone or in pairs.

...or cormorant?

Cormorants often
spread-eagle on posts.

Common Loon

hooked bill

black body

Double-Crested Cormorant

Mute swan...or whistling swan?

Swans, like geese and puddle ducks, feed on plants and seeds. They often turn tail-up in the water but they don't dive under it. The mute swan was brought to North America from Europe. Although it's beautiful, it's called an invader, because it often chases out native birds. You can tell a mute swan by its orange bill.

The whistling swan is a native swan, sometimes called the tundra swan. Spot this wild swan as it migrates through the Great Lakes. You can tell a wild swan by its black bill.

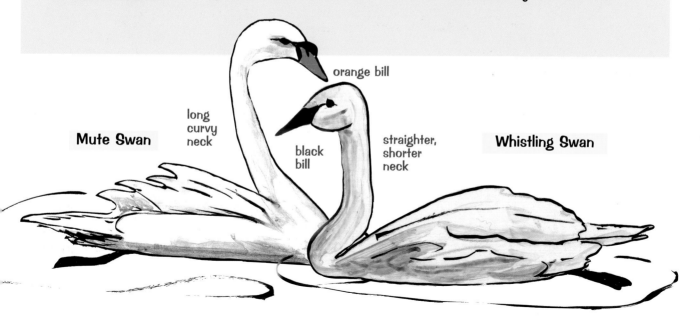

orange bill

long curvy neck

Mute Swan

black bill

straighter, shorter neck

Whistling Swan

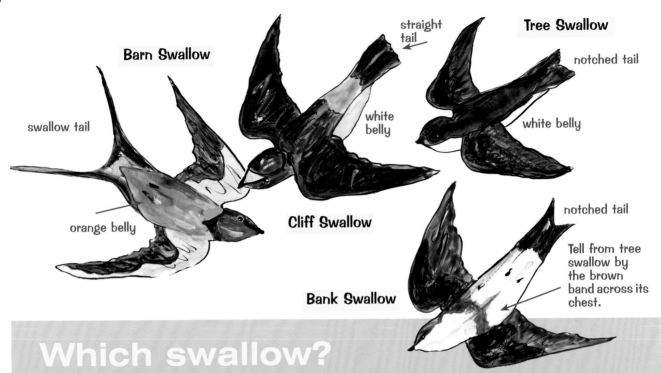

Barn Swallow

swallow tail

orange belly

straight tail

white belly

Cliff Swallow

Tree Swallow

notched tail

white belly

notched tail

Tell from tree swallow by the brown band across its chest.

Bank Swallow

Which swallow?

Several kinds of hand-sized swallows flit low over the water, especially in the early evening. Swallows swoop so fast after flying insects that it may be hard to tell one from another. Their tails differ, though, and so do their homes. Bank swallows can make a sand bank look like a big piece of swiss cheese. Cliff swallows glue their mud-jug homes under bridges or lighthouse walkways. Barn swallows prefer inside places like barns, sheds, or empty buildings. Tree swallows often nest near water in dead trees.

Sandpiper...or killdeer?

Many skinny-legged shorebirds prowl the water's edge. The robin-sized killdeer and spotted sandpiper are two easy ones to spot. The killdeer bobs its head, has two big stripes on its chest, and cries "Kill-DEEEE." The spotted sandpiper bobs the back end of its body, has spots on its chest, and cries "Pea-weet!" Some people call it a "teeter tail."

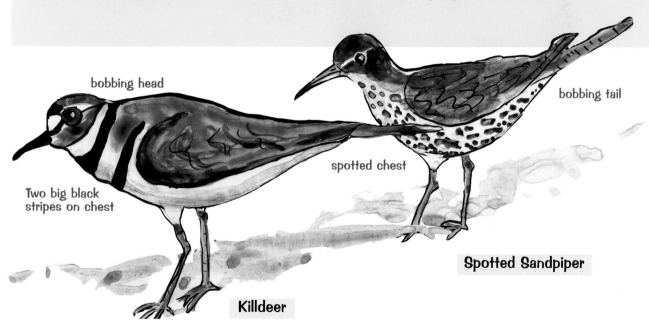

bobbing head

bobbing tail

spotted chest

Two big black
stripes on chest

Spotted Sandpiper

Killdeer

big black and white hawk-like bird

Osprey...

Because the osprey eats fish, it's sometimes called a fish eagle. It hovers and dives like a tern. Watch it carry off its catch head-first between its claws.

fish

Osprey

white head

white tail

Bald Eagle

curly plume

S-curved neck, even while flying

Great Blue Heron

...or eagle?

The adult bald eagle's huge size, white head, and white tail make it an easy bird to spot. It scoops fish from near the water's surface. Watch for it soaring on thermals like a gull, or perched at the tip of a tall tree like a great blue heron.

Heron, crane...

Three of the biggest birds on the Great Lakes fish or feed along shorelines and in wet marshy places. All three stand tall on long skinny legs. The white egret is easy to recognize. Look for the great blue heron on treetops or fishing alone along a shore. Sandhill cranes gather in noisy crowds. Wings spread wide, they sometimes leap high and dance.

...or egret?

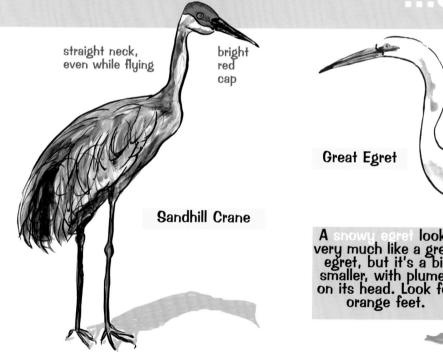

straight neck, even while flying

bright red cap

Sandhill Crane

white body and head

Great Egret

A snowy egret looks very much like a great egret, but it's a bit smaller, with plumes on its head. Look for orange feet.

Toad...

Toads prefer dry land. Two kinds of toads hop along Great Lakes shores—the American toad and Fowler's toad. Each toad has a white line down the middle of its back. You won't get warts from touching a toad, but you might hurt the toad's thin skin.

white line down middle of its back

Bullfrog

dark leg stripes

Frogs like water. Tell the greenish bullfrog by the dark stripes on its legs and its deep, BOING-BOING croak. Look for bullfrogs perched on logs or lily pads.

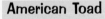

American Toad

...or frog?

Eastern Hognose Snake

wide head and neck

tightly curled tail

Hognose, water snake...
...or rattler?

Two splotchy-looking snakes live around beaches. You can easily tell them apart by looking at both ends. The northern water snake has a narrow head and tail. It can be bad-tempered, but it's not poisonous. The hognose snake has a wide snout and a curly pig-like tail. The hognose snake may hiss, but it's harmless. Don't mistake it for the eastern Massasauga rattlesnake, which is almost never seen on beaches. A rattlesnake has a wide, heart-shaped head, narrow neck, and rattles on its tail. It's best to leave snakes alone.

narrow head

Northern Water Snake

rattles on tail

big heart shaped head

narrow pointed tail

Eastern Massasauga Ratllesnake

Painted turtle...or snapping turtle?

Find Great Lakes turtles in quiet waters. Painted turtles pile up on logs, sunning. Look for the beautiful red designs around the shell edges. A snapping turtle, often alone, can grow very big. Be careful—it moves fast and can bite hard! Tell a snapping turtle by its long, spiky, dinosaur-like tail and hooked upper jaw. There are not so many turtles around the Great Lakes any more. Be a friend to a turtle—leave it in its home.

hooked
upper jaw

Snapping Turtle

jagged
long tail

Painted Turtles

red design at edge of shell

Who lived there?

The homes of underwater creatures often wash up on Great Lakes shores. Some, like the little striped zebra mussels that clump up on almost everything, are invaders and are not welcome. If you pick up a shell and somebody is still at home, put it back in the lake!

Crayfish claw

Mussel

Zebra Mussel

Crayfish bodies

Snail

Pretty things...

Look for eye-catching treasures that wash up on the beach: feathers from gulls and waterbirds, brightly colored pieces of glass made smooth by sand and water, and driftwood in beautiful shapes.

Sedimentary rock...

An igneous rock was once lava from an ancient volcano. Made by fire, it's so hard that you can't scratch it with a nail. A sedimentary rock is formed by layers of sand, mud, or mineral. It's soft enough to scratch with a nail.

Identifying beach stones is difficult, but you can look for a few easy ones. Find the best stones in the rain, which brightens the colors, or just after storm waves throw new stones onto the beach.

sedimentary rock

igneous rock

...or igneous?

Sandstone

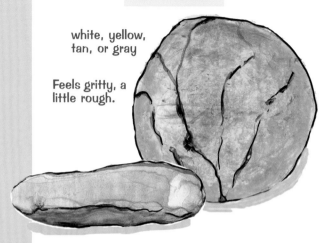

white, yellow, tan, or gray

Feels gritty, a little rough.

white, yellow, tan, or pink

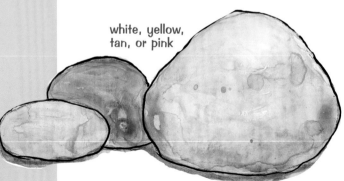

Smooth, sometimes lets light through it.

Quartz

Basalt

black or
blue-gray

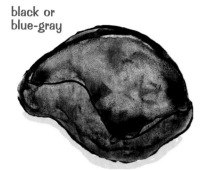

smooth, sometimes even silky

Granite

light colors, flecked
with black, pink, or
gray

hard, jagged, or smooth

If it's too frustrating to
find a stone you can name,
look for colors or special
shapes. Heart shapes, for
example, are common in
nature. Try hunting for stones
with natural holes in them.
Some people call these "lucky
stones." String them on a cord for
a necklace.

colored stripes—often more than
two colors...very beautiful!

smooth and very hard

Agate

whitish or light gray

smooth, but soft enough
to scratch with a nail

Limestone

Heart-shaped stone

Stone with a hole

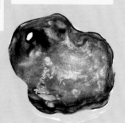

Brachiopods are usually two shells clamped together. This is the empty space made by a brachiopod.

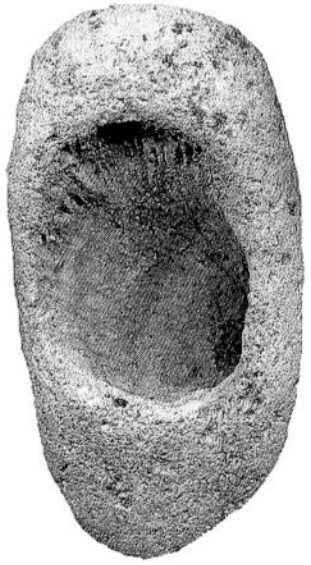

Brachiopod

Dinophyllum

light chains on darker stone

Chain Coral

Sometimes the disks are stuck together in a tube. Often the hole in the middle is closed.

tube

disks with holes

Clam Fossil

Photo by Richard A. Paselk. Used with permission.

Crinoids

net-like
pattern

Honeycomb Coral

snake-skin
pattern

Petoskey Stone

Which ancient creature?

You can often find plants and creatures that are millions of years old hiding in Great Lakes stones. Find clams, mollusks, snails, lots of corals, parts of other animals, and many kinds of plants. Sometimes all you can see is the shape of a creature that once was there.

The fossils on this page are shown actual size, but they can be larger or smaller. Often they look like common gray stones until they become wet. Rainy days offer great fossil hunting.

Hint: Rub your stones or fossils with hand lotion to deepen the color and make them shine for a long time.

How many toes?

Because so many mammals don't sneak out to the water's edge until dark, you are more likely to see their tracks than the animals themselves. Reading tracks is a skill, but you can often tell some of them by counting toes.

A one-toe track is a horse's hoof. Two-toe tracks are probably made by deer or moose hooves. Three-toed tracks are birds—webbed tracks are made by swimmers, and nonwebbed by shore or other birds.

Dogs, cats, hares, and rabbits have four toes. Many mammals, like you, have five. Some, like the mouse, have five toes in back (hind) and four in front (fore).

Snake Trail

1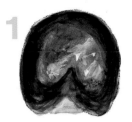
Horse

2
Moose

2
Deer

3
Waterbird

3
Gull or Tern

3
Crow

3
Shorebird

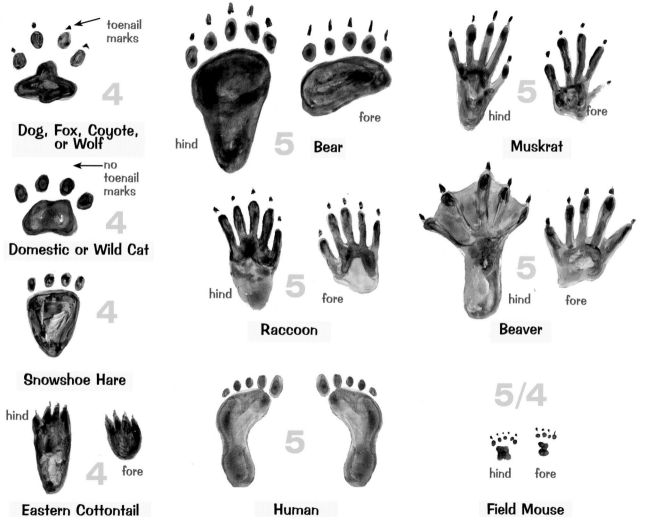

toenail marks

4

Dog, Fox, Coyote, or Wolf

no toenail marks

4

Domestic or Wild Cat

4

Snowshoe Hare

hind

fore

4

Eastern Cottontail

hind

5

fore

Bear

hind

5

fore

Raccoon

hind

fore

Muskrat

hind

5

fore

Beaver

5

Human

5/4

hind   fore

Field Mouse

Sedge... ...or grass?

Do you think that all grasses look alike? Look again! Many kinds of grasses grow on Great Lakes beaches. The most important is beach grass, also called marram grass. It grows in clumps connected by underground stems, which help keep the sand from blowing away. Giant reedgrass is an invader. Although its big feathery plumes are beautiful, giant reedgrass is taking over many marshes.

A grass-like plant with a triangle-shaped stem is a sedge.

hard, knobby flower head

Grows up to 15 feet tall!

triangular cross-sec-tion of the stem

Grows in water in vast numbers.

Underground stems connect clumps.

Porcupine Sedge

Beach Grass

Giant Reedgraas

Cattail or horsetail?

Cattails are the supermarket of wetland beaches—almost every part can be eaten by something! Watch for flower heads shaped like hot dogs that later become fluffy.

Horsetails contain silicon. It makes them rough and good for scrubbing pots on camping trips. Bulrushes are plants without leaves. Look for them growing in water.

spiky tops

fresh flower head

old flower head

Christmas tree shape

no leaves

drooping brown flower clusters

Grows in water.

Cattail

Common Horsetail

Bulrush

How does it smell?

Color may be the first thing you notice about a wildflower, but it's not the only clue to what kind of flower it is. Some wildflowers—like milkweed, yarrow, and tansy—have strong or unusual smells.

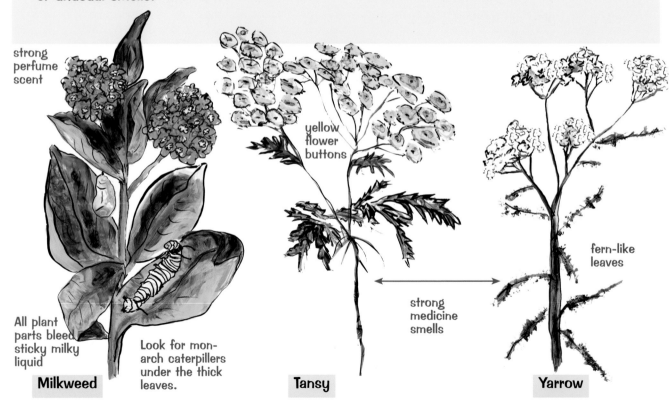

strong perfume scent

yellow flower buttons

fern-like leaves

All plant parts bleed sticky milky liquid

strong medicine smells

Look for monarch caterpillers under the thick leaves.

Milkweed

Tansy

Yarrow

How high or low?

Plants which grow unusually high or low are especially easy to spot. Bearberry and silver-weed spread low across the sand. Silverweed sends out red shoots to start new plants. Bearberry shrubs look tough, but some are very old and should not be walked on. Mullein is a high plant. It can grow tall as a child!

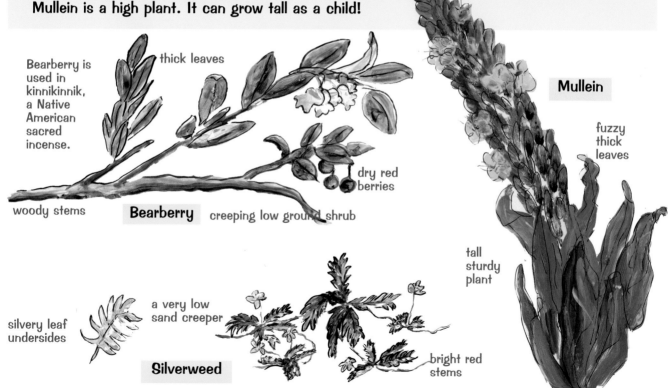

Bearberry is used in kinnikinnik, a Native American sacred incense.

thick leaves

Mullein

fuzzy thick leaves

dry red berries

woody stems

Bearberry   creeping low ground shrub

tall sturdy plant

silvery leaf undersides

a very low sand creeper

Silverweed

bright red stems

Should I pick it?

You'll be sorry if you pick poison ivy! Just a touch makes many people break into an itchy rash. Some wildflowers are becoming rare and should not be picked. Wildflowers feed many kinds of wildlife. Seeds that are not eaten might mean more wildflowers next year. Sometimes picking a flower can kill the plant. Why not leave wildflowers where you find them?

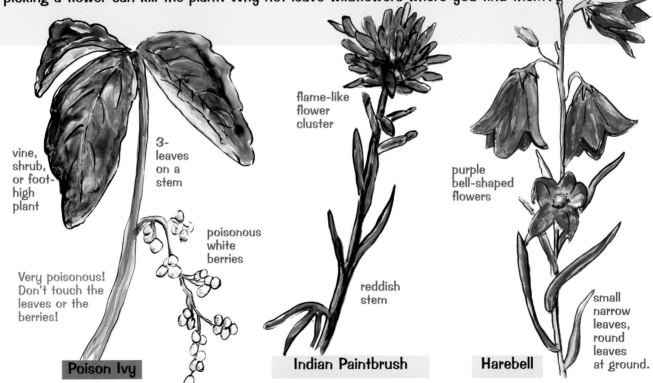

vine, shrub, or foot-high plant

3-leaves on a stem

flame-like flower cluster

purple bell-shaped flowers

poisonous white berries

Very poisonous! Don't touch the leaves or the berries!

reddish stem

small narrow leaves, round leaves at ground.

Poison Ivy

Indian Paintbrush

Harebell

Blooms in
the evening.

Evening Primrose

Blooms in
sunlight.

four big
fringed
petals

Fringed Gentian

When does it bloom?

All plants react to light, but some of them are more sensitive than others. The evening primrose closes during the day and opens in the evening. The lovely fringed gentian will only bloom in bright light, curling up like an umbrella on dark days.

Round spots like these are called **eyespots.**

Buckeye

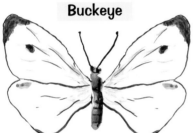

Cabbage Butterfly

Clouded Sulphur

Tiger Swallowtail

Pointed bottom wings are called **swallowtails.**

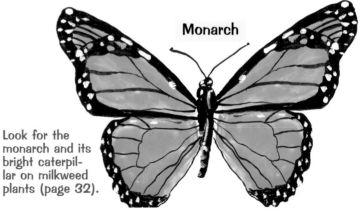

Monarch

Look for the monarch and its bright caterpillar on milkweed plants (page 32).

Red Admiral

These two butterflies are about the same size. They often appear together.

Painted Lady

Lady...or admiral?

The beach is a special place for butterflies, which can show up in large numbers. A few—like the monarch, red admiral, and painted lady—migrate along Great Lakes shores. If caught in a storm, they sometimes wash up on the beach. When they dry off, they may fly away.

Swallowtails are the biggest beach butterflies. Their size and fancy tails make them look like butterfly superstars. The tiger swallowtail is just one of many swallowtails.

Don't kill these beauties. Butterflies should be free.

eyespots

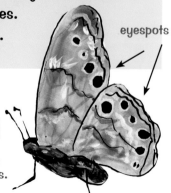

Northern Pearly Eye

This is just one of many brown spotted butterflies.

Dragonfly, damselfly...

All kinds of beautiful damselflies and dragonflies brighten wet beaches on sunny days. It's easy to tell which is which when they are perched on something: a damselfly rests with wings folded. A dragonfly rests with wings spread.

The antlion burrows in the sand, popping out to snag ants. Later it turns into a winged flyer. It's hard to see, though, as the antlion adult flutters its wings at night.

...or antlion?

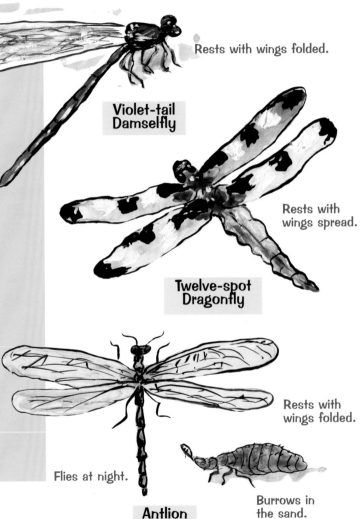

Rests with wings folded.

Violet-tail Damselfly

Rests with wings spread.

Twelve-spot Dragonfly

Rests with wings folded.

Flies at night.

Antlion

Burrows in the sand.

Will it bite me?

real size

Mosquito

Bites!

Doesn't bite!

You probably don't think that some of these creatures are treasures. They are, though, even if some of them bite. Most beach insects attract and feed all sorts of wonderful fish and birds.

It's hard to miss a big loud horsefly or deerfly buzzing around your head. Black flies, lady bugs, and sand flies often show up in big daytime numbers. Mosquitoes and mayflies are thickest at night.

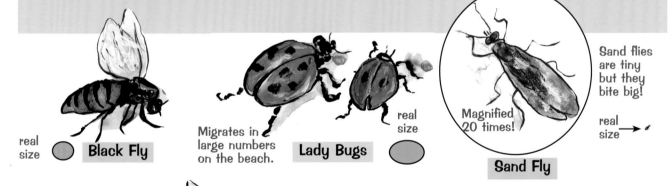

real size **Black Fly**

Migrates in large numbers on the beach.

Lady Bugs

real size

Magnified 20 times!

Sand flies are tiny but they bite big!

real size →

Sand Fly

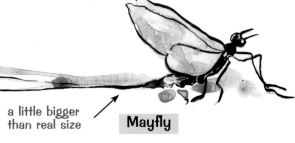

a little bigger than real size

Mayfly

Flies around and around your head!

A deerfly looks and acts much like a horsefly.

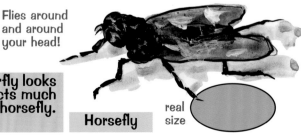

Horsefly

real size

It's time to go treasure-hunting on this sandy beach.
How many of these birds, wildflowers, insects,
animals, and grasses can you name?
Find the answers on page 48.

Now go treasure hunting on a wetland beach.
How many of these birds, insects, animals, and plants can you name?
Find the answers on page 48.

Index

Sandhill Crane

Answer Page

What's on pages 42–43?

bank swallows	cormorants	loons	spotted sandpiper
beach grass	eagle	mergansers, female	tansy
buckeye	harebells	mergansers, male	tree swallow
bufflehead, female	herring gulls	mullein	yarrow
buffleheads, male	hognose snake	mute swans	
Caspian terns	killdeer	ring-billed gull	
common terns	lady bugs	silverweed	

What's on pages 44–45?

black tern	coots	horsetails	painted turtles
Bonaparte's gulls	damselfly	Indian paintbrush	porcupine sedge
bullfrog	dragonfly	milkweed	sandhill crane
bulrushes	gentians	mallards	snapping turtle
Canada geese	great egrets	northern pearly eye	toad
cattails	giant reedgrass	northern water snake	whistling swans
cliff swallows	heron	ospreys	wood duck

These are the islands shown on the map on page 5. Most of these are part of a group of islands, called an archipeligo.

○ U.S. Island

○ Canadian Island

1 Isle Royale

2 Apostle Islands

3 Grand Island

4 Beaver Island

5 Fox Islands

6 Manitou Islands

7 Washington Island

8 Drummond Island

9 Mackinac Island

10 Manitoulin Island

11 Bois Blanc Island

12 South Bass Island

13 Wolfe Island